percussion

essential Musicianship

for band

ADVANCED

ensemble concepts

Eddie Green
John Benzer
David Bertman

Percussion by
Evelio Villarreal

Unit

1	Establishing Sound	2
2	Establishing Articulation	6
3	Linear Intervals Created Up and Down	24
4	Vertical Intervals Created Up and Down	28
5	Note Lengths	40
6	Creating Intervals with a Pedal Tone	70
7	Extending Skills in Lower Register	98
8	Extending Skills in Upper Register	103
9	Combining Elements	109
10	Learning to Play Cadences	118
11	Learning Even Note-Valued Technique	119

Percussion Basics 120

Glossary Concepts, Terms and Techniques 142

ISBN 978-0-634-08853-7

HAL•LEONARD®
CORPORATION
7777 W. BLUEMOUND RD. P.O. BOX 13819 MILWAUKEE, WI 53213

1. Establishing Sound

1–1 Block Concert F

 Percussion Goals

Level 1
1. Breathe together.
2. Start together.
3. Strike the instrument in the same place, with the same **energy**, every time.
4. Rolls should be smooth and even, without extraneous noise.

Level 2/3
P   1.   Snare drum roll speed (16th note, 8th note or 16th note triplet base) should be determined by the tempo.

 Percussion Goals (1–2)

Level 1
1. Breathe together.
2. Start together.
3. Strike the instrument in the same place, with the same **energy**, every time.
4. All strokes should have a smooth beginning, middle and end.
5. Where applicable, dampen to **match** the ends of the wind players' notes.
6. Match the articulation style/dynamic level of the wind players.

Level 2/3
P   1.   Snare drum roll speed (16th note, 8th note or 16th note triplet base) will be determined by tempo of the exercise.

Boldface words are terms that can be found in the glossary at the back of the book.

Goal Key: **P**=Snare, Bass Drum and Cymbals; **K**=Keyboard; **A**=Auxiliary; **T**=Timpani

ⓜ = Muffle (dampen)

1–2 Concert F – Non-Touching Notes
(Goals on p.2)

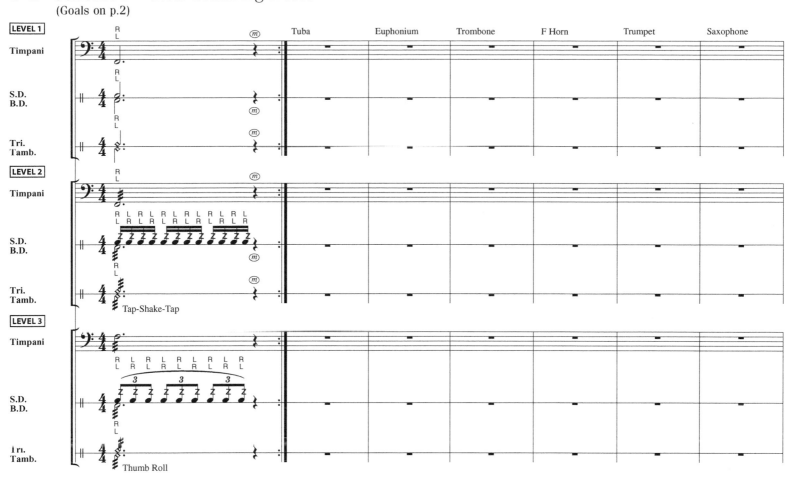

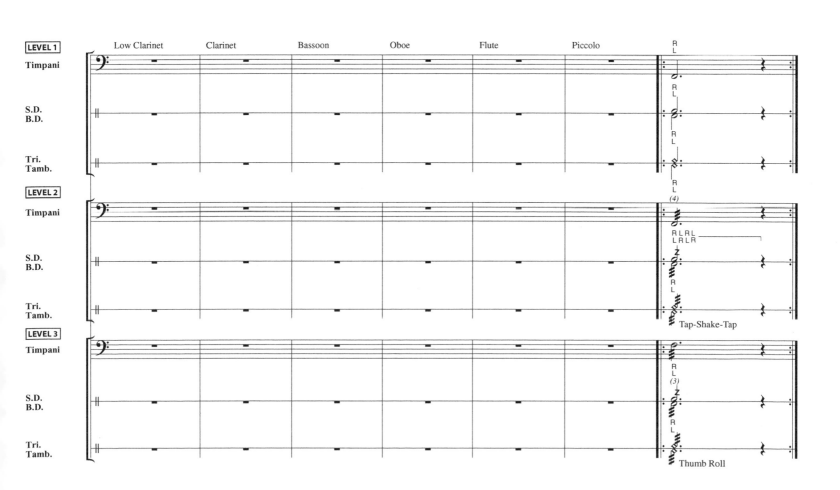

1–3   Concert F – Touching Notes

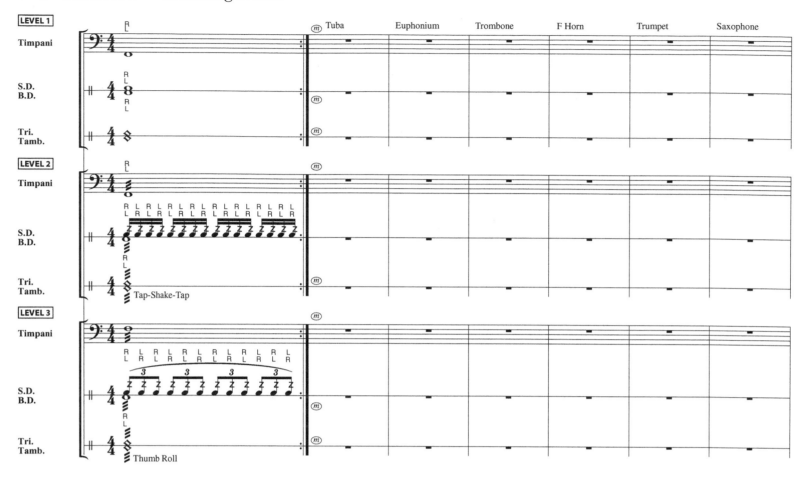

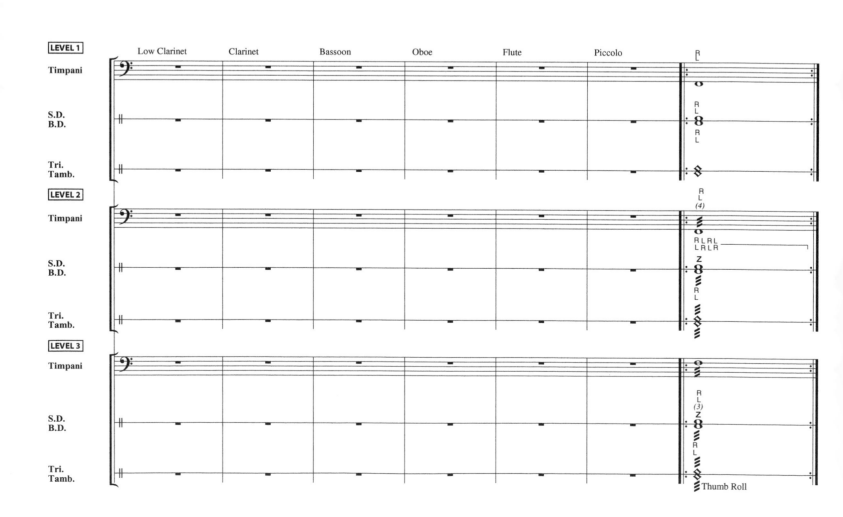

Percussion Goals

Level 1

1. Breathe together.
2. Start together.
3. Strike the instrument in the same place, with the same **energy**, every time.
4. Where applicable, dampen to **match** the ends of the wind players' notes.
5. Do not accent the beginnings of rolls.
6. Hands, wrists and arms should look natural and feel soft and relaxed.

Level 2/3

A   1. Tambourine and triangle rolls should be smooth, without accents at the beginning or end.

1–4 Color Drill   P<small>ERCUSSION</small> T<small>ACET</small>

2. Establishing Articulation

2–1 Articulation Drill – Long To Short Note Values

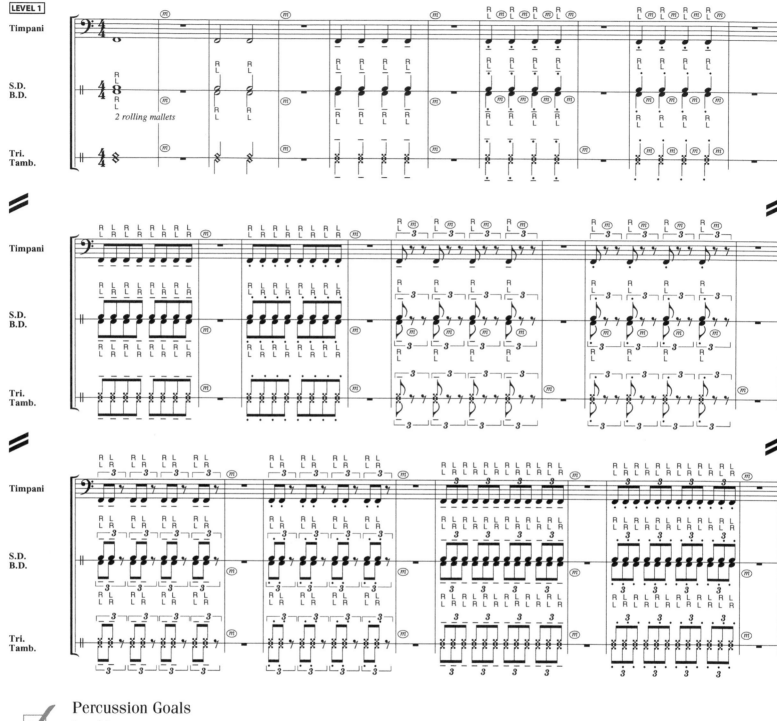

 Percussion Goals

Level 1

1. Breathe together.
2. Start together.
3. Strike the instrument in the same place, with the same **energy** every time.
4. **Match** the articulation style of the wind players.
5. Where applicable dampen with the ends of the wind players' notes, where applicable.
6. Return the mallets/sticks to their starting position during rests ("**musical silence**") and at the end of the exercise.
7. Posture should be natural with the body position balanced. The body and face should remain still.
8. The quicker the notes, the smoother the mallets/sticks should look. The mallets/sticks should move WITH the hands, NOT as a reaction to that movement.
9. As the metronome produces new subdivisions, they should be "**internalized**."
10. Breathe on count 3 during whole rests.

K,T 11. When applicable, use appropriate pedaling and dampening to match the articulation length of the wind players.

Boldface words are terms that can be found in the glossary at the back of the book.

Goal Key: **P**=Snare, Bass Drum and Cymbals; **K**=Keyboard; **A**=Auxiliary; **T**=Timpani

* This is the first occurrence where the metronome should produce different subdivisions within the exercise.

ⓜ = Muffle (dampen)

2–1 Articulation Drill – Long To Short Note Values (*cont.*)

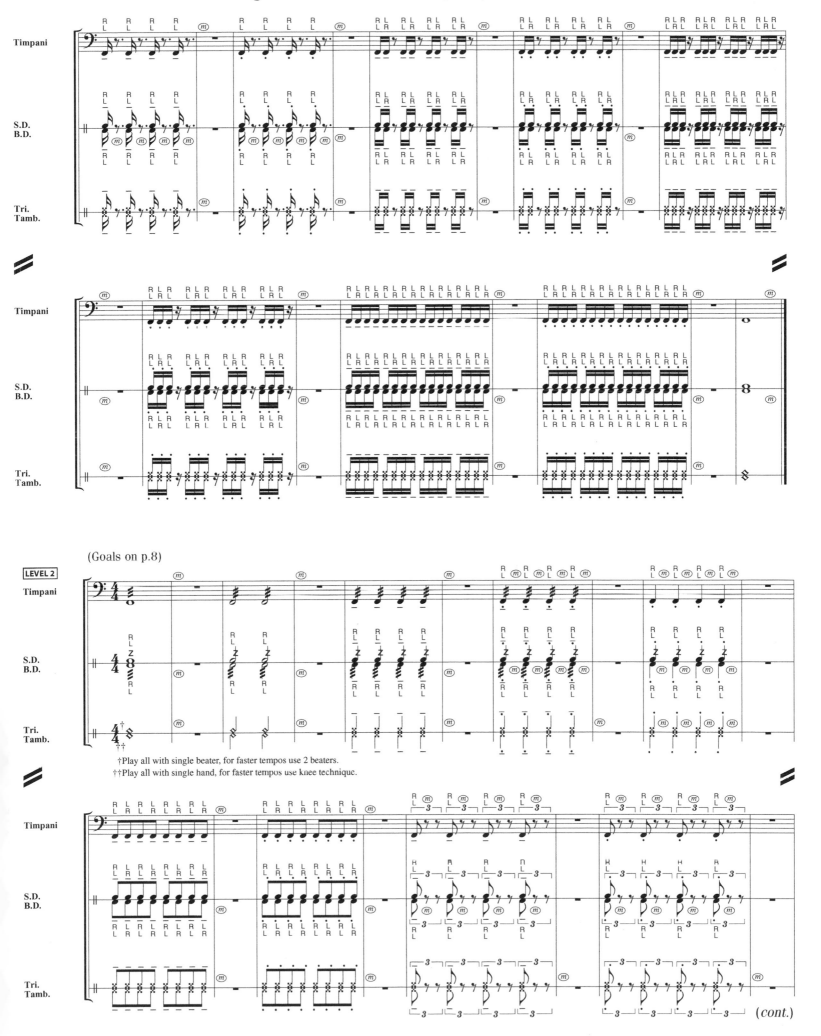

†Play all with single beater, for faster tempos use 2 beaters.
††Play all with single hand, for faster tempos use knee technique.

(Goals on p.8)

(*cont.*)

2–1 Articulation Drill – Level 2 (*cont.*)

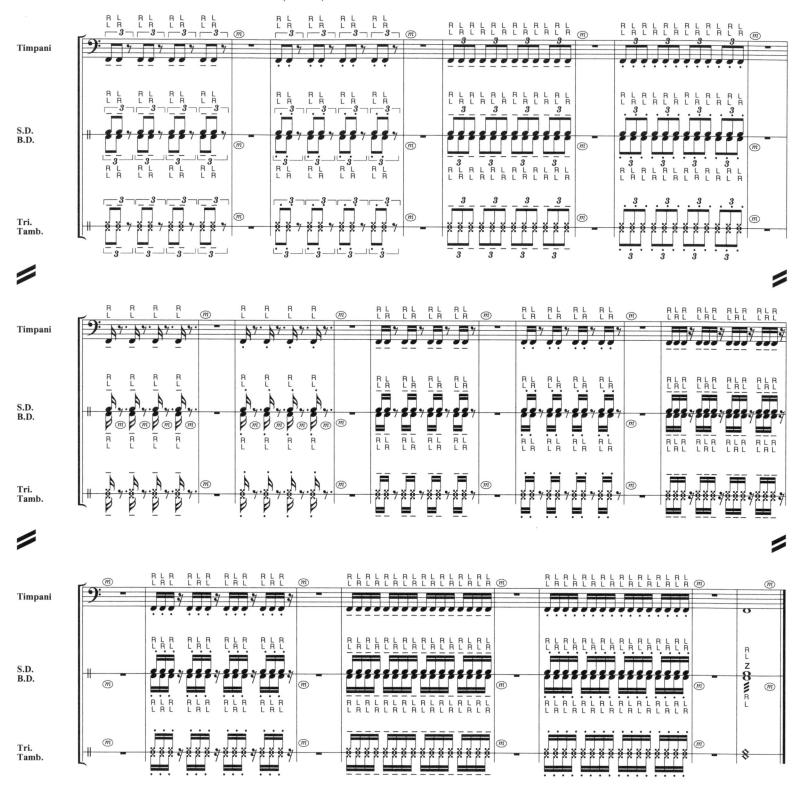

Percussion Goals
Level 2/3

P	1.	All flams should have the same quality of sound.
P	2.	Do not accent the beginnings of rolls.
P	3.	Bass drum mallet position on the head should be slightly different from rolls (towards edge) to single strokes (towards center) for clarity.
P	4.	Snare drum hand motion should look the same from single strokes to bounces.
A	5.	When using two triangle beaters, they should be made of the same material and have the same weight.
K,T	6.	Rolls should be smooth and even, without extraneous noise.

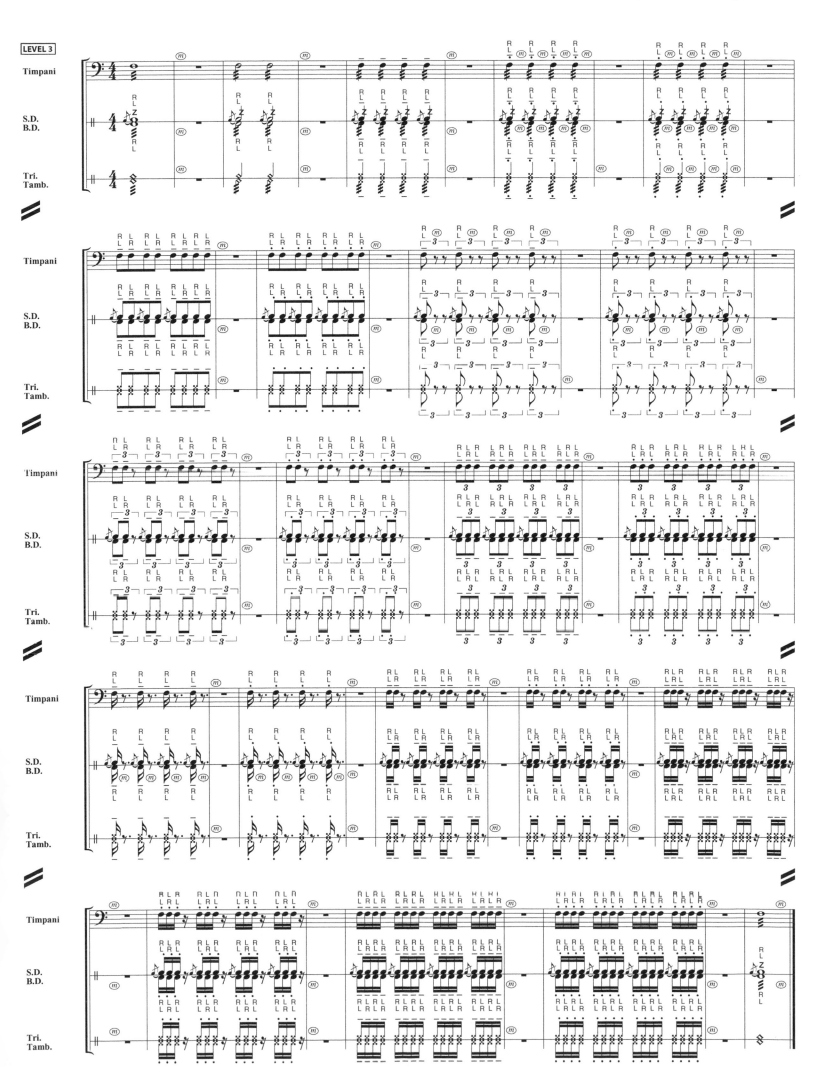

2–2 Articulation Drill – Short to Long Note Values
(Goals on p.13)

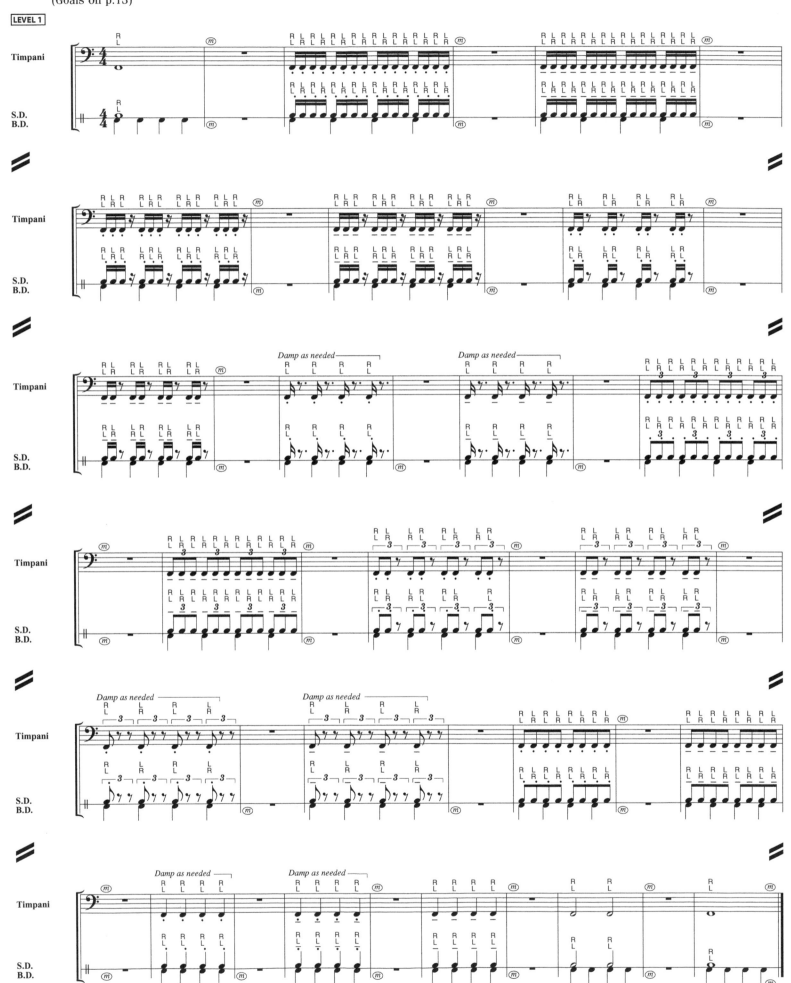

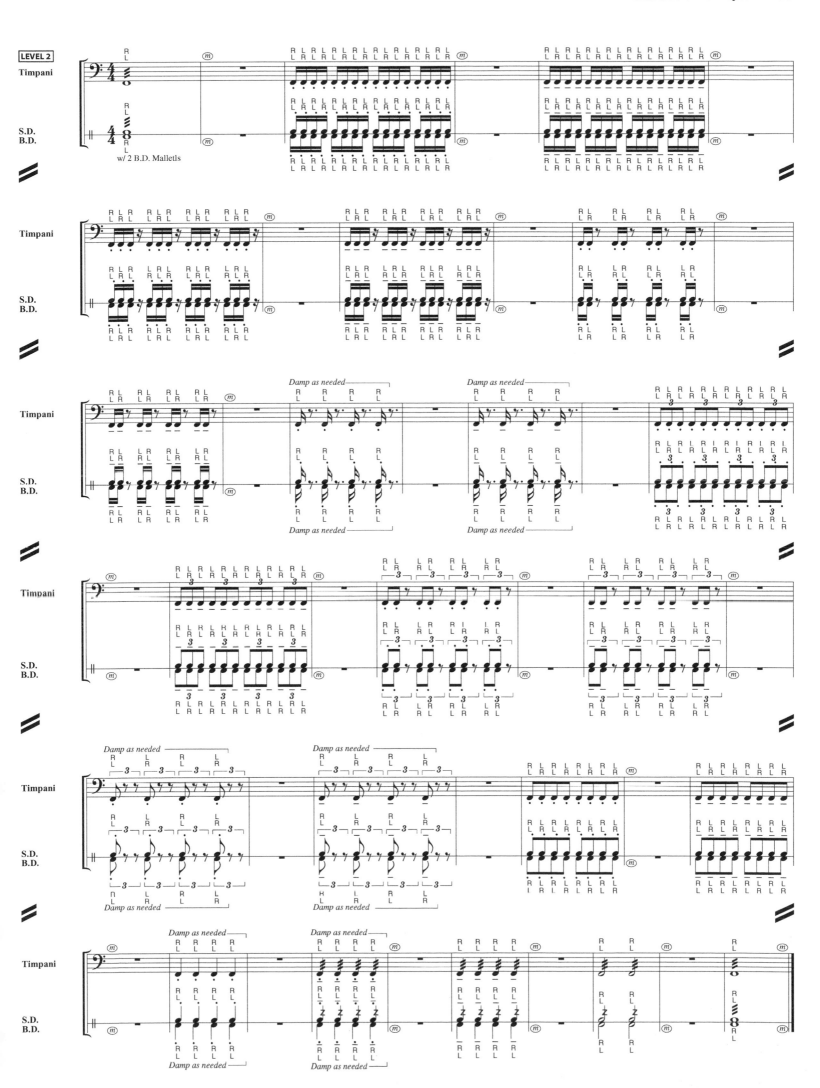

2–2 Articulation Drill – Short to Long Note Values (*cont.*)

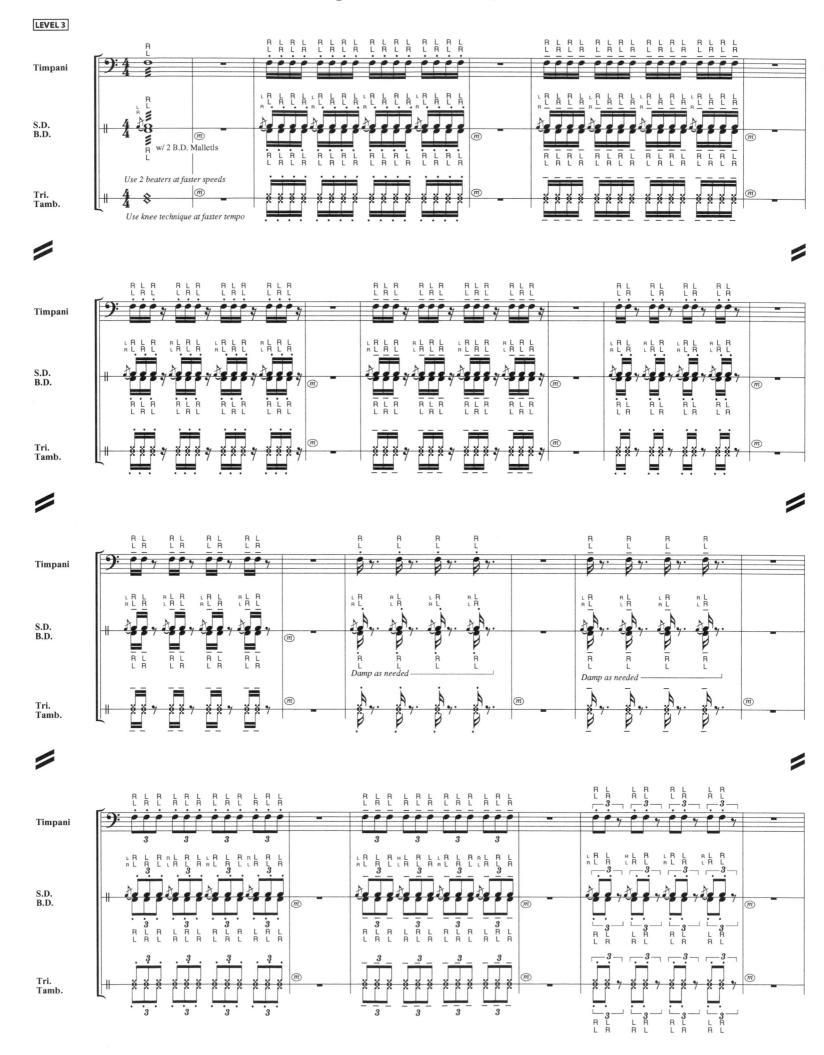

 Percussion Goals

Level 1
1. Breathe together.
2. Start together.
3. Strike the instrument in the same place, with the same **energy** every time.
4. **Match** the articulation style of the wind players.
5. Return the mallets/sticks to their starting position during rests ("**musical silence**") and at the end of the exercise.
6. Posture should be natural with the body position balanced. The body and face should remain still.
7. Hands, wrists and arms should look natural and feel soft and relaxed.
8. The quicker the notes, the smoother the mallets/sticks should look. The mallets/sticks should move WITH the hands, NOT as a reaction to that movement.
9. As the metronome produces new subdivisions, they should be "**internalized**."
10. Breathe on count 3 during whole rests.

K,T 11. When applicable, use appropriate pedaling and dampening to match the articulation length of the wind players.

Level 2/3
P 1. All flams should have the same quality of sound.
P 2. Bass drum mallet position on the head should be slightly different from rolls (towards edge) to single strokes (towards center) for clarity.
P 3. Snare drum hand motion should look the same from single strokes to bounces.
A 4. When using two triangle beaters, they should be made of the same material and have the same weight.
K,T 5. Do not accent the beginnings of rolls.
K,T 6. Rolls should be smooth and even, without extraneous noise.

2–3 Articulation Drill – Long to Short Note Values

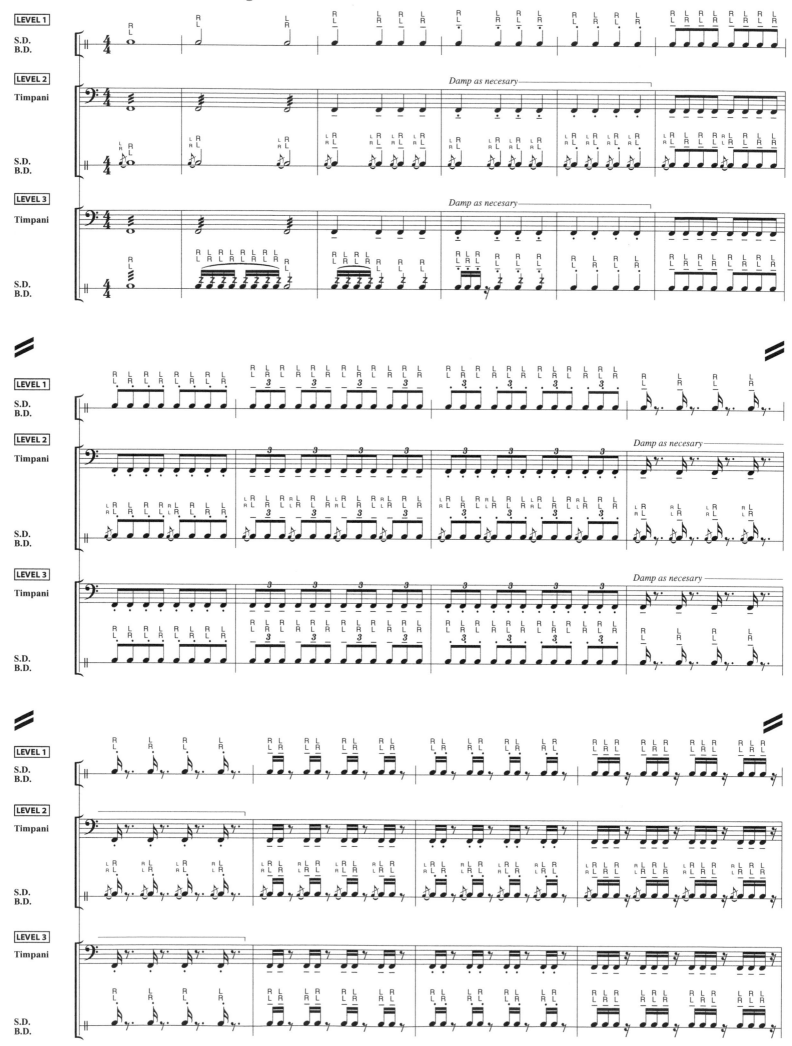

Percussion Goals

Level 1
1. Breathe together.
2. Start together.
3. Strike the instrument in the same place, with the same **energy** every time.
4. **Match** the articulation style of the wind players.
5. Return the mallets/sticks to their starting position during rests ("**musical silence**") and at the end of the exercise.
6. Posture should be natural with the body position balanced. The body and face should remain still.
7. The stroke beginnings and ends should be smooth (touch-lift strokes).
8. Hands, wrists and arms should look natural and feel soft and relaxed.
9. The quicker the notes, the smoother the mallets/sticks should look. The mallets/sticks should move WITH the hands, NOT as a reaction to that movement.
10. The body should not move during rests.

Level 2/3
P,K,T 1. Do not accent the beginnings of rolls.
P 2. All flams should have the same quality of sound throughout.
P 3. Snare drum hand motion should look the same from single strokes to bounces.
K,T 4. Rolls should be smooth and even, without extraneous noise.
K,T 5. Where applicable, dampen where necessary to **match** te ends of the wind players' notes.

2–4 Articulation Control Exercise – Long to Short Note Values

 ## Percussion Goals

Level 1

1. Breathe together.
2. Start together.
3. Strike the instrument in the same place, with the same **energy** every time.
4. **Match** the articulation style of the wind players.
5. Where applicable, dampen with the ends of the wind players' notes.
6. Posture should be natural with the body position balanced. The body and face should remain still.
7. The stroke beginnings and ends should be smooth (touch-lift strokes).
8. Hands, wrists and arms should look natural and feel soft and relaxed.
9. The quicker the notes, the smoother the mallets/sticks should look. The mallets/sticks should move WITH the hands, NOT as a reaction to that movement.
10. Breathe on count 4 quarter rests.

K,T 11. When applicable, use appropriate pedaling and dampening to match the articulation length of the wind players.

Level 2/3

P,K,T 1. Rolls should be smooth and even, without extraneous noise.

P 2. All flams should have the same quality of sound.

K,T 3. Do not accent the beginnings of rolls.

2–5 Articulation Control Exercise – Short to Long Note Values

 Percussion Goals

Level 1

1. Breathe together.
2. Start together.
3. Strike the instrument in the same place, with the same **energy** every time.
4. **Match** the articulation style of the wind players.
5. Posture should be natural with the body position balanced. The body and face should remain still.
6. The stroke beginnings and ends should be smooth (touch-lift strokes).
7. Hands, wrists and arms should look natural and feel soft and relaxed.
8. The quicker the notes, the smoother the mallets/sticks should look. The mallets/sticks should move WITH the hands, NOT as a reaction to that movement.
9. Breathe on count 4 quarter rests.

K,T 10. When applicable, use appropriate pedaling and dampening to match the articulation length of the wind players.

Level 2/3

P,K,T 1. Rolls should be smooth and even, without extraneous noise.

K,T 2. Do not accent the beginnings of rolls.

2–6 Pick-Up Note Drill #1 (Ascending)

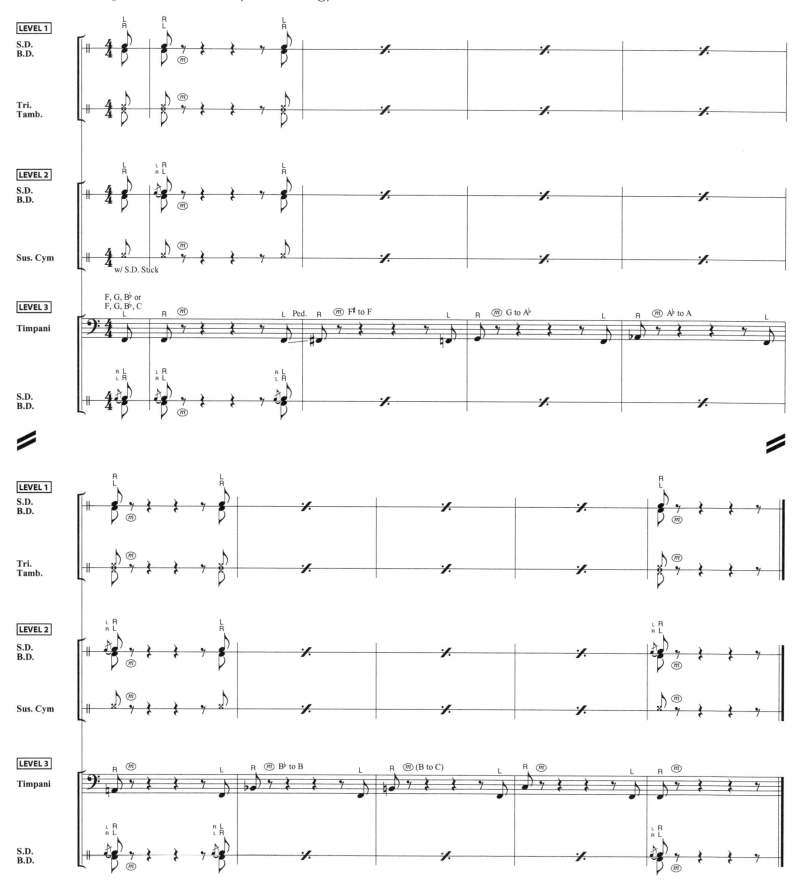

 ### Percussion Goals

1. All pick-up notes should have the same **tonal energy** as the following note.
2. Each pick-up note should have the same **strength**.
3. Each pick-up note should have forward motion toward the downbeat. The exception to this rule is when the downbeat note is a higher **pitch** than the pick-up note(s).
4. All pick-up notes should be the same length.
5. Preparatory counts will be given for this exercise.

2–7 Pick-Up Note Drill #2 (Ascending)

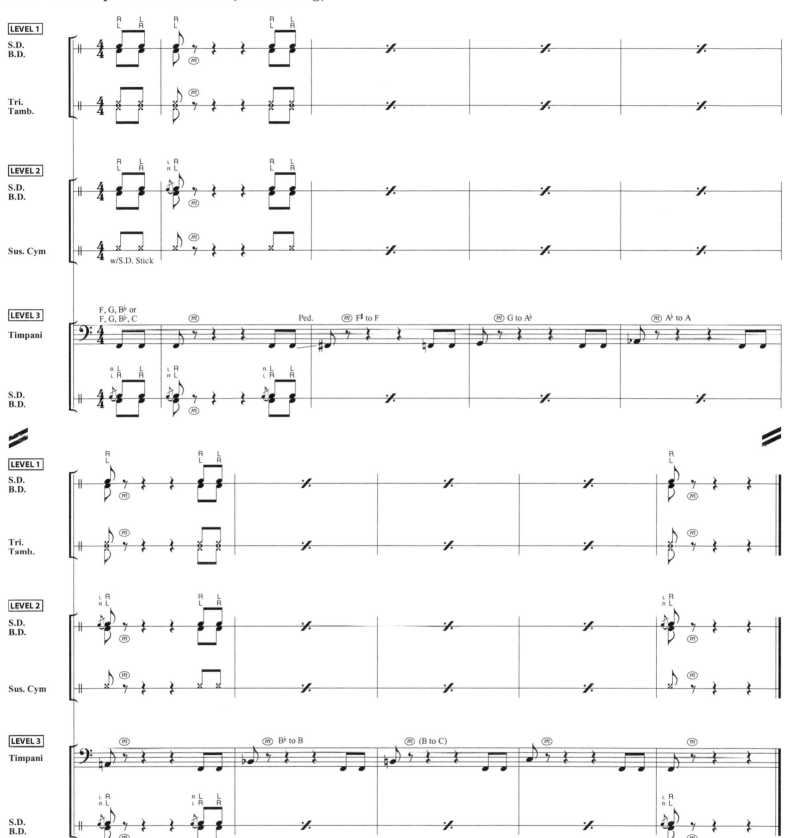

 ## Percussion Goals
Level 1
 1. All pick-up notes should have the same **tonal energy** as the following note.
 2. Preparatory counts will be given for this exercise.
 3. Breathe on each count 3.

Level 2/3
P 1. All flams should have the same quality of sound.
K 2. Notes played in octaves should sound at exactly the same time; subdivide internally.
T 3. Pedaling should occur (fast) just before the mallet strikes the head.

2–8 Pick-Up Note Drill #3 (Ascending)

  Percussion Goals

Level 1

1. All pick-up notes should have the same **tonal energy** as the following note.
2. Preparatory counts will be given for this exercise.
3. Breathe on each count 2.

Level 2/3

P 1. All flams should have the same quality of sound.

K 2. Notes played in octaves should sound at exactly the same time; subdivide internally.

T 3. Pedaling should occur (fast) just before the mallet strikes the head.

2–9 Pick-Up Note Drill #1 (Descending)

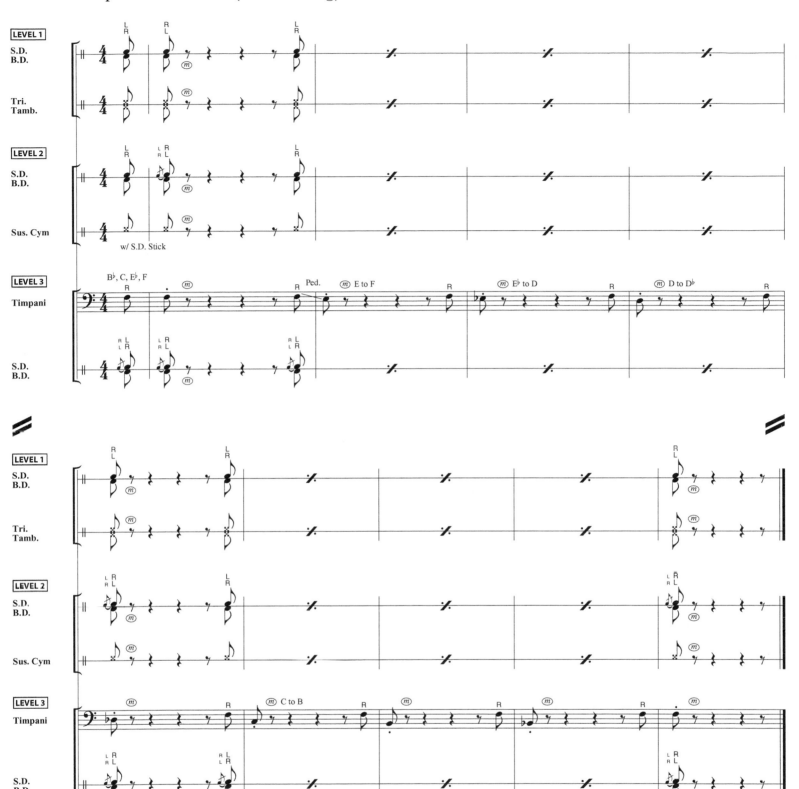

 Percussion Goals

Level 1

1. All pick-up notes should have the same **tonal energy** as the following note.
2. Each pick-up note should have forward motion toward the downbeat. Exception: downbeat notes that are higher **pitches** than the pick-up note should not sound stronger than the pick-up note.
3. Preparatory counts will be given for this exercise.

Level 2/3

P 1. All flams should have the same quality of sound.

K 2. Notes played in octaves should sound at exactly the same time; subdivide internally.

T 3. Pedaling should occur (fast) just before the mallet strikes the head.

2–10 Pick-Up Note Drill #2 (Descending)

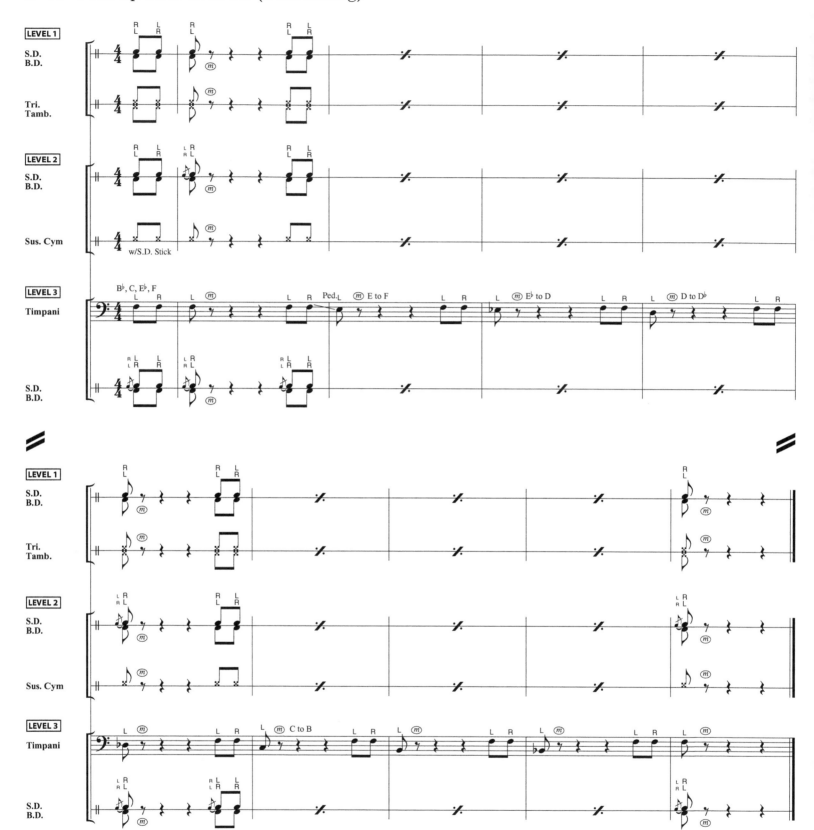

 ### Percussion Goals

Level 1

1. All pick-up notes should have the same **tonal energy** as the following note.
2. Each pick-up note should have forward motion toward the downbeat. Exception: downbeat notes that are higher **pitches** than the pick-up note should not sound stronger than the pick-up note.
3. Preparatory counts will be given for this exercise.

Level 2/3

P 1. All flams should have the same quality of sound.

K 2. Notes played in octaves should sound at exactly the same time; subdivide internally.

T 3. Pedaling should occur (fast) just before the mallet strikes the head.

2–11 Pick-Up Note Drill #3 (Descending)

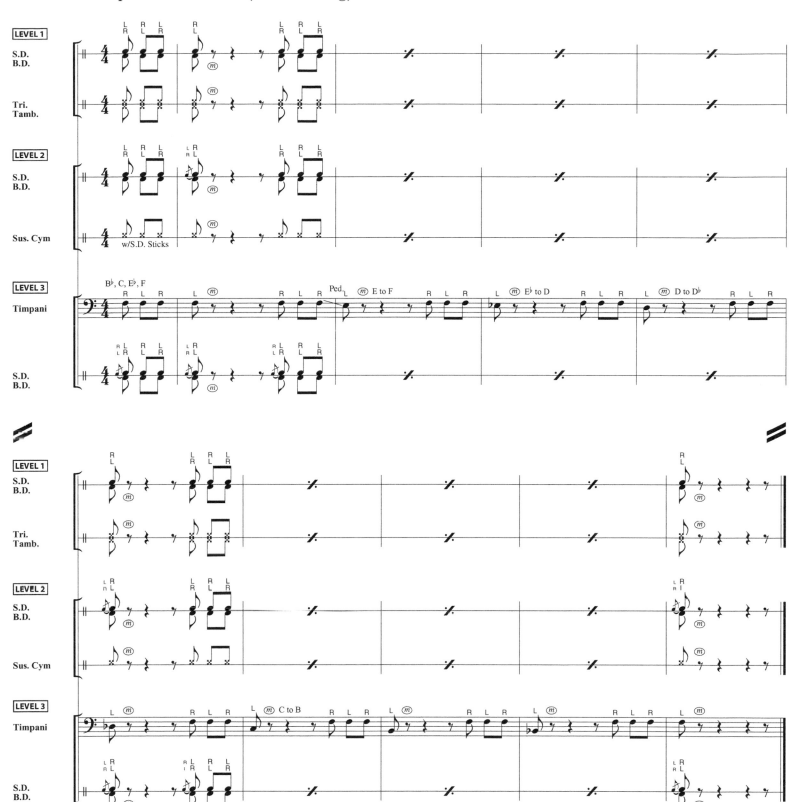

 Percussion Goals

Level 1
1. All pick-up notes should have the same **tonal energy** as the following note.
2. Each pick-up note should have forward motion toward the downbeat. Exception: downbeat notes that are higher **pitches** than the pick-up note should not sound stronger than the pick-up note.
3. Preparatory counts will be given for this exercise.

Level 2/3
P 1. All flams should have the same quality of sound.
K 2. Notes played in octaves should sound at exactly the same time; subdivide internally.
T 3. Pedaling should occur (fast) just before the mallet strikes the head.

3. Linear Intervals Up and Down

3-1 Descending Intervals Created Up and Down

Percussion Goals

Level 1

1. Breathe together.
2. Start together.
3. Strike the instrument in the same place, with the same **energy** every time.
4. Where applicable, dampen to **match** the ends of the wind players' notes.
5. Match the articulation style of the wind players.
6. The middle note of each group should match the surrounding notes in tone and volume.
7. Breathe on count 4 quarter rests.
8. This exercise can be practiced with single strokes or rolls.

Level 2/3

P   1. All flams and ruffs should have the same quality of sound throughout.
P   2. Snare drum roll speed (16th note, 8th note, 16th note triplet base) should be determined by the tempo.
K,T 3. Rolls should be smooth and even, without extraneous noise.

Boldface words are terms that can be found in the glossary at the back of the book.

Goal Key: **P**=Snare, Bass Drum and Cymbals; **K**=Keyboard; **A**=Auxiliary; **T**=Timpani

ⓜ = Muffle (dampen)

3–2 Ascending Intervals

Percussion Goals

Level 1

1. Breathe together.
2. Start together.
3. Strike the instrument in the same place, with the same **energy** every time.
4. Where applicable, dampen to **match** the ends of the wind players' notes.
5. The middle note of each group should match the surrounding notes in tone and volume.
6. The third note of each group should match the **tonal energy** of the first note.
7. Breathe on count 4 quarter rests.
8. This exercise can be practiced with single strokes or rolls.

Level 2/3

P	1.	All flams and ruffs should have the same quality of sound throughout.
P	2.	Snare drum roll speed (16th note, 8th note, 16th note triplet base) should be determined by the tempo.
K	3.	Notes played in octaves should sound at exactly the same time; subdivide internally.
K	4.	When playing rolls in octaves, they should be tonally even, hand-to-hand.
K,T	5.	Rolls should be smooth and even, without extraneous noise.

4. Vertical Intervals Created Up and Down

4–1   Expanding Interval Flow Drill

Percussion Goals

Level 1

    1.   Breathe together.

    2.   Start together.

    3.   Strike the instrument in the same place, with the same **energy** every time.

    4.   Where applicable, dampen to **match** the ends of the wind players' notes.

    5.   Match the articulation style/dynamic level of the winds.

    6.   Rolls should be smooth and even, without extraneous noise.

    7.   The middle note of each group should match the surrounding notes in tone and volume.

    8   The third note of each group should match the **tonal energy** of the first note.

    9.   As intervals expand, lead with the proper hand (left/down, right/up).

   10.   Breathe on count 4 quarter rests.

P   11.   Snare drum hand motion should look the same from single strokes to bounces.

Level 2

P   1.   Rolls should have smooth beginnings and ends, without extraneous noise.

K   2.   Octave rolls should be consistent note-to-note and have smooth beginnings and ends without extraneous noise.

K   3.   Notes played in octaves should sound at exactly the same time; subdivide internally.

Boldface words are terms that can be found in the glossary at the back of the book.

Goal Key: **P**=Snare, Bass Drum and Cymbals; **K**=Keyboard; **A**=Auxiliary; **T**=Timpani

4–2 Expanding Interval Flow Drill – Non-Touching Notes (Model and Ensemble)

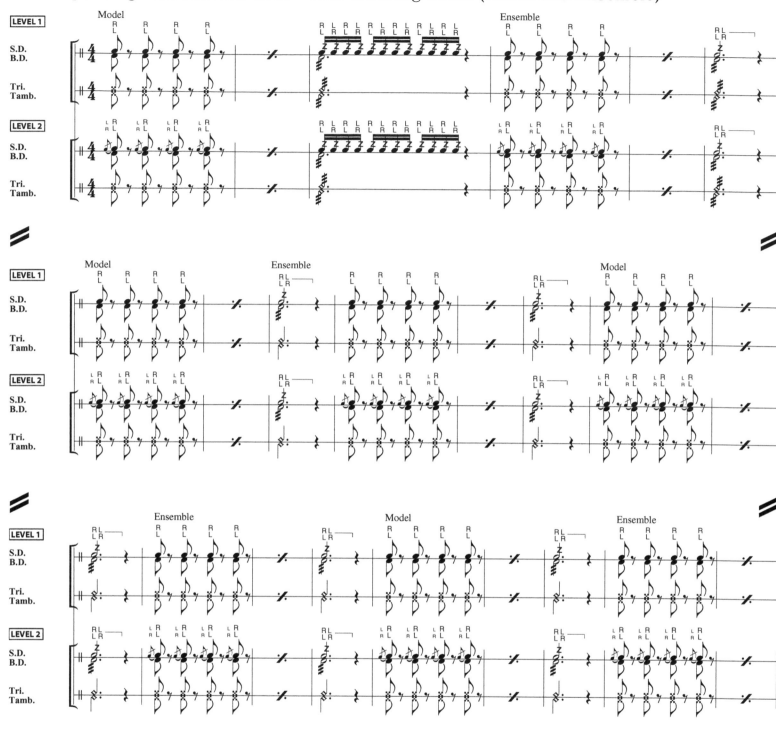

 Percussion Goals

Level 1

1. Breathe together.
2. Start together.
3. Strike the instrument in the same place, with the same **energy** every time.
4. Where applicable, dampen to **match** the ends of the wind players' notes.
5. Match the articulation style/dynamic level of the winds.
6. The middle note of each group should match the surrounding notes in tone and volume.
7. The third note of each group should match the **tonal energy** of the first note.
8. As intervals expand, lead with the proper hand (left/down, right/up).
9. Breathe on count 4 quarter rests.
P 10. Snare drum hand motion should look the same from single strokes to bounces.

Level 2

P 1. Rolls should have smooth beginnings and ends, without extraneous noise.
P 2. All flams and ruffs should have same quality of sound throughout.
K 3. Octave rolls should be consistent note-to-note and have smooth beginnings and ends without extraneous noise.
K 4. Notes played in octaves should sound at exactly the same time; subdivide internally.

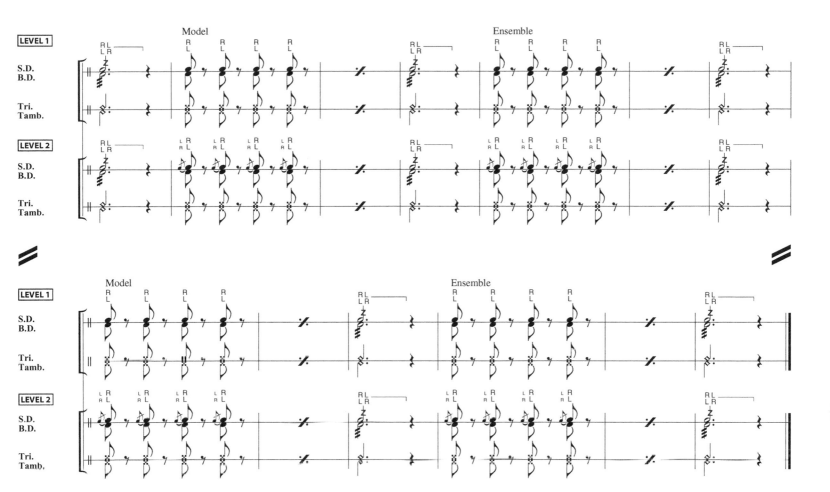

4–3 Expanding Interval Flow Drill – Touching Notes (Model and Ensemble)

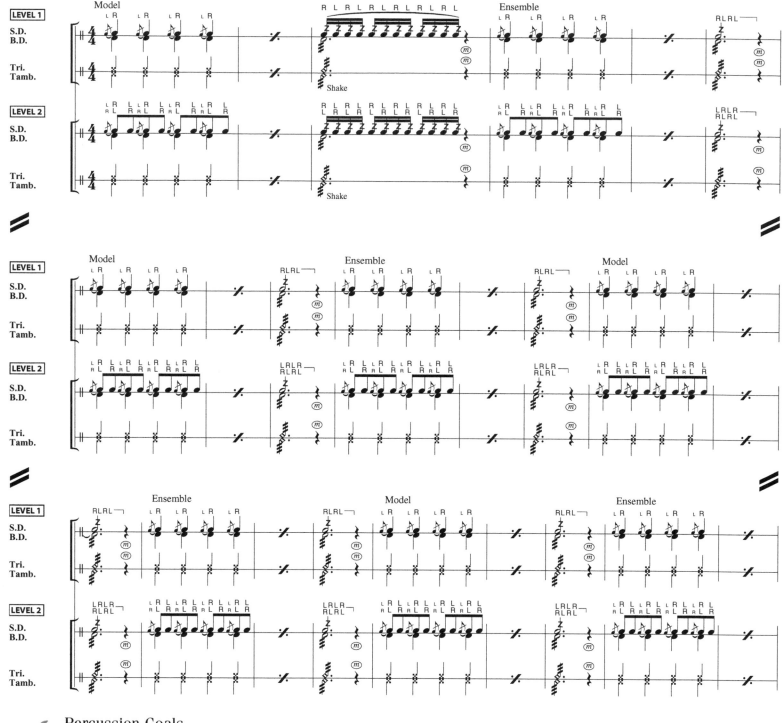

Percussion Goals

Level 1

1. **Match** the articulation style/dynamic level of the winds.
2. Strike the instrument in the same place, with the same **energy**, every time.
3. Where applicable, dampen to match the ends of the wind players' notes.
4. Rolls should be smooth and even, without extraneous noise.
5. Posture should be a natural, balanced body position, with shoulders sloped and relaxed.
6. Hand, wrist and arm movement should be smooth and fluid.
7. Snare drum hand motion should look the same from single strokes to bounces.
8. Breathe on count 4 quarter rests.
  P 9. All flams should have the same quality of sound throughout.
  P 10. Snare drum stroke height should be consistent when playing rolls.
  P 11. Snare drum roll speed (16th note, 8th note, 16th note triplet base) should be determined by the tempo.

Level 2

  P 1. Rolls should have smooth beginnings and ends, without extraneous noise.
  P 2. All flams and ruffs should have same quality of sound throughout.
  K 3. Octave rolls should be **balanced** note-to-note and have smooth beginnings and ends with no extraneous noise.
  K 4. Notes played in octaves should sound at exactly the same time; subdivide internally.

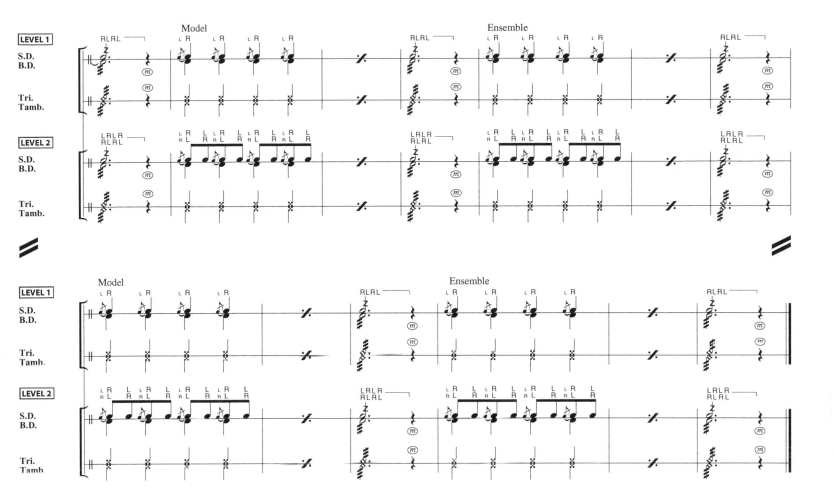

4–4 Parallel Interval Flow Drill – Touching Half Notes (Model and Ensemble)

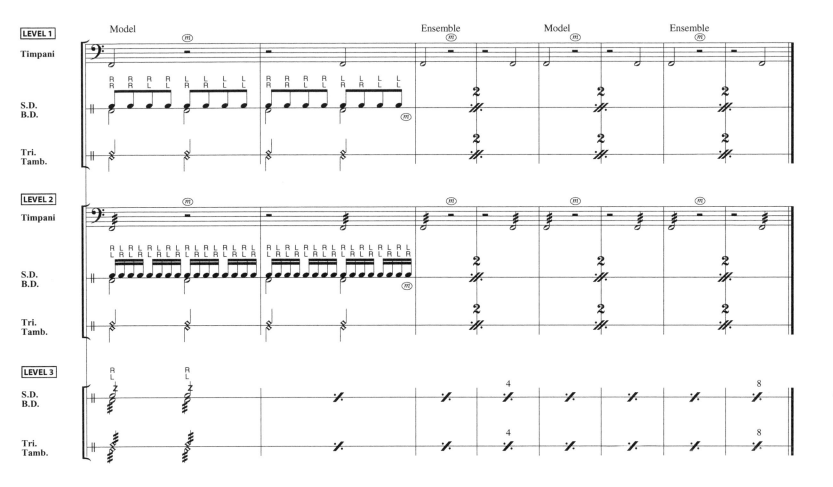

 Percussion Goals

Level 1
1. Breathe together.
2. Start together.
3. Release together.
4. **Match energy**/dynamic level of the winds.
5. Strike the instrument in the same place, with the same energy, every time.
6. Where applicable, dampen to match the ends of the wind players' notes.
7. Hand, wrist and arm movement should be smooth and fluid.
8. Snare drum hand motion should look the same from single strokes to bounces.
9. Notes should have a consistent tonal **resonance** throughout.
P 10. Snare drum stroke height should be consistent when playing rolls.

Level 2/3
P,K 1. Rolls should be smooth and even, without extraneous noise.
K 2. Notes played in octaves should sound at exactly the same time; subdivide internally.

4–5 Parallel Interval Flow Drill – Non-Touching Notes (Model and Ensemble)

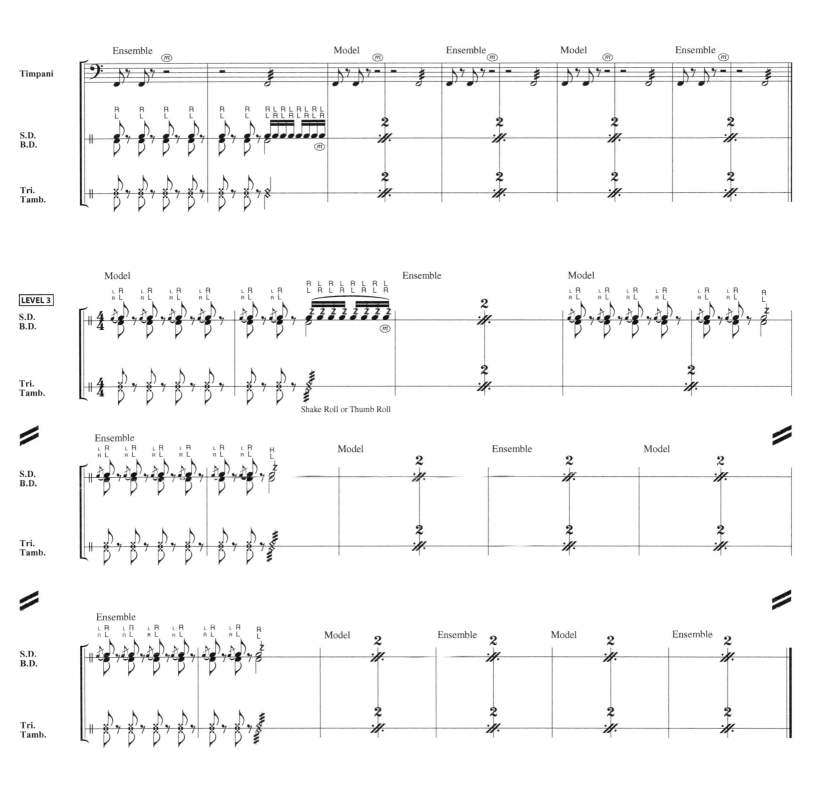

Percussion Goals

Level 1

1. **Match** the articulation style/dynamic level of the winds.
2. Strike the instrument in the same place, with the same **energy**, every time.
3. Where applicable, dampen to match the ends of the wind players' notes.
4. Hand, wrist and arm movement should be smooth and fluid.
5. Posture should be a natural, balanced body position, with shoulders sloped and relaxed.
6. Snare drum hand motion should look the same from single strokes to bounces.
7. Stroke height should be the same hand-to-hand and stroke-to-stroke.
8. Notes should have a consistent tonal **resonance** throughout.

Level 2/3

P   1. Rolls should have smooth beginnings and ends, without extraneous noise.
P   2. All flams and ruffs should have same quality of sound throughout.
K   3. Octave rolls should be **balanced** note-to-note and have smooth beginnings and ends with no extraneous noise.
K   4. Notes played in octaves should sound at exactly the same time; subdivide internally.

4–6 Parallel Interval Flow Drill – Touching Quarter Notes (Model and Ensemble)

 Percussion Goals

Level 1

1. **Match** the articulation style/dynamic level of the winds.
2. Strike the instrument in the same place, with the same **energy**, every time.
3. Where applicable, dampen to match the ends of the wind players' notes.
4. Hand, wrist and arm movement should be smooth and fluid.
5. Posture should be a natural, balanced body position, with shoulders sloped and relaxed.
6. Snare drum hand motion should look the same from single strokes to bounces.
7. Stroke height should be the same hand-to-hand and stroke-to-stroke.
8. Notes should have a consistent tonal **resonance** throughout.
9. The ensemble should sound as clear as the **model**.

5. Note Lengths

5–1 Ascending Combined Skill Drill – Non-Touching Notes (Model and Ensemble)

 Percussion Goals

Level 1

1. Breathe together.
2. Start together.
3. Strike the instrument in the same place, with the same **energy** every time.
4. Where applicable, dampen to **match** the ends of the wind players' notes.
5. Match the articulation style/dynamic level of the winds.
6. Posture is a natural, balanced body position with shoulders sloped and relaxed.
7. Do not accent the beginnings of rolls.
8. Rolls should be smooth and even, without extraneous noise.
9. Hands, wrists and arms should look natural and feel soft and relaxed.

Level 2/3

P 1. All ruffs should have the same quality of sound throughout.

Boldface words are terms that can be found in the glossary at the back of the book.

Goal Key: **P**=Snare, Bass Drum and Cymbals; **K**=Keyboard; **A**=Auxiliary; **T**=Timpani

Ⓜ = Muffle (dampen)

5–2 Descending Combined Drill – Non-Touching Notes

 Percussion Goals (for 5–2, 5–3 and 5–4)

Level 1
1. **Match** the articulation style/dynamic level of the winds.
2. Where applicable, dampen to match the ends of the wind players' notes.
3. Posture should be a natural, balanced body position, with shoulders sloped and relaxed.
4. Each stroke should be smooth and natural.
5. Hands, wrists and arms should look natural and feel soft and relaxed.
6. Notes should have a consistent tonal **resonance** throughout.
7. Breathe on count 4 quarter rests.

Level 2/3
P   1.   All flams and ruffs should have the same quality of sound throughout.
P   2.   Snare drum roll speed (16th note, 8th note, 16th note triplet base) should be determined by the tempo.
K   3.   Notes played in octaves should sound at exactly the same time; subdivide internally.
P,K,T 4.   Rolls should be smooth and even, without extraneous noise.

5–3 Ascending Combined Skill Drill – Touching Notes (Model and Ensemble)
(Goals on p.43)

5–4 Descending Combined Skill Drill – Touching Notes (Model and Ensemble)
(Goals on p.43)

5–5 Style Exercise – Perfect Fifths/Long to Short Note Values

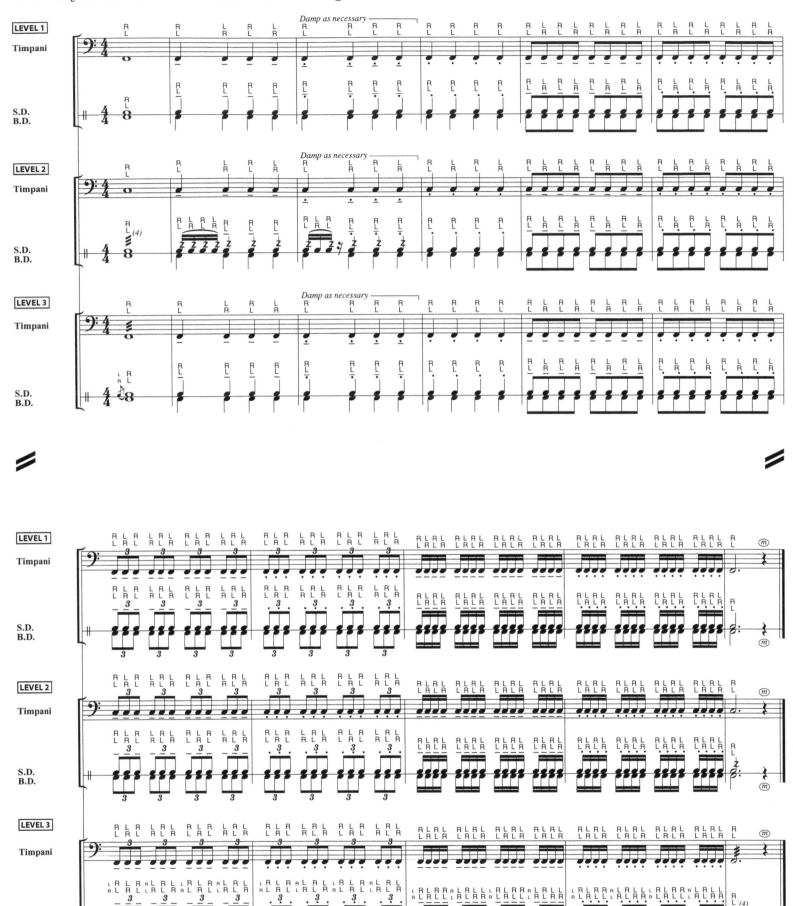

Percussion Goals

Level 1

1. Breathe together.
2. Start together.
3. Strike the instrument in the same place, with the same **energy** every time.
4. **Match** the articulation style of the wind players.
5. Posture should be natural with the body position balanced. The body and face should remain still.
6. The stroke beginnings and ends should be smooth (touch-lift strokes).
7. Hands, wrists and arms should look natural and feel soft and relaxed.
8. The quicker the notes, the smoother the mallets/sticks should look. The mallets/sticks should move WITH the hands, NOT as a reaction to that movement.
9. Breathe on count 4 quarter rests.

K,T 10. When applicable, use appropriate pedaling and dampening to match the articulation length of the wind players.

Level 2/3

P 1. All flams should have the same quality of sound.

K,T 2. Do not accent the beginnings of rolls.

P,K,T 3. Rolls should be smooth and even, without extraneous noise.

5–6 Style Exercise – Perfect Fifths/Non-Changing Notes

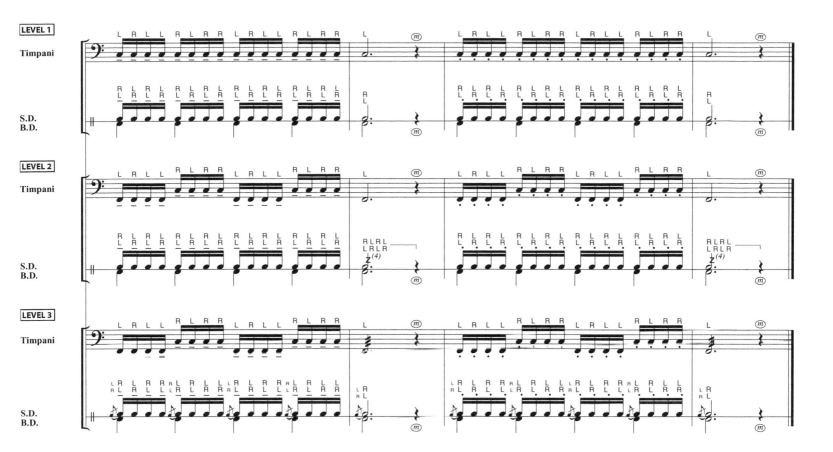

 Percussion Goals

Level 1

1. Breathe together.
2. Start together.
3. **Match** the articulation style of the wind players.
4. Release together.
5. Posture should be natural with the body position balanced. The body and face should remain still.
6. Use appropriate pedaling and dampening to match length of notes of the wind players.
7. Strike the instrument in the same place, with the same **energy** every time.
8. Hands, wrists and arms should look natural and feel soft and relaxed.
9. The notes should not weaken as rhythms become more active.
10. Breathe on count 4 quarter rests
11. All parts are interchangeable, but should remain in **balance** throughout.
12. Each note should not be louder or softer than the note preceding it.

Level 2/3

P	1.	All flams should have the same quality of sound.
P	2.	As rhythms become more active, they should not get louder or softer.
K,T	3.	As pitches ascend, the higher note should not be louder than the lower note.
K,T	4.	As pitches descend, the lower note should not be softer than the higher note.
P,K,T	5.	Rolls should be smooth and even, without extraneous noises.

5–7 Style Exercise – Perfect Fourths/Non-Changing Notes

Percussion Goals

Level 1
1. Breathe together.
2. Start together.
3. **Match** the articulation style of the wind players.
4. Release together.
5. Posture should be natural with the body position balanced. The body and face should remain still.
6. Use appropriate pedaling and dampening to match length of notes of the wind players.
7. Strike the instrument in the same place every time.
8. Hands, wrists and arms should look natural and feel soft and relaxed.
9. The notes should not weaken as rhythms become more active.
10. Breathe on count 4 quarter rests
11. All parts are interchangeable, but should remain in **balance** throughout.
12. Each note should not be louder or softer than the note preceding it.

Level 2/3
P	1.	All flams should have the same quality of sound.
P	2.	As rhythms become more active, they should not get louder or softer.
K,T	3.	As pitches ascend, the higher note should not be louder than the lower note.
K,T	4.	As pitches descend, the lower note should not be softer than the higher note.
P,K,T	5.	Rolls should be smooth and even, without extraneous noises.

5-8 Style Exercise – Major Thirds/Non-Changing Notes

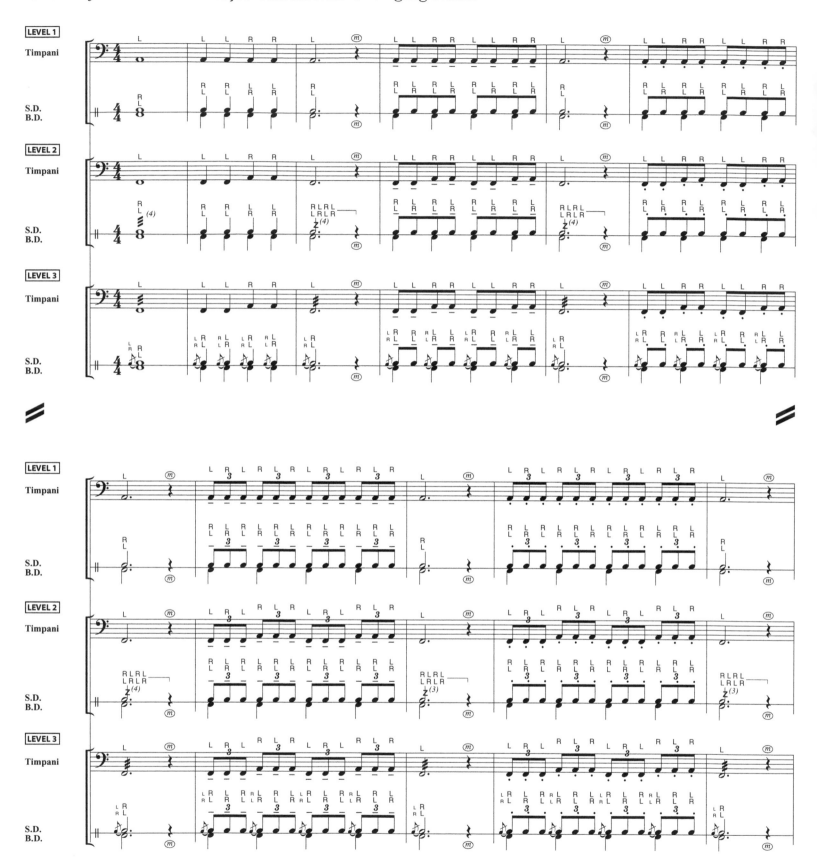

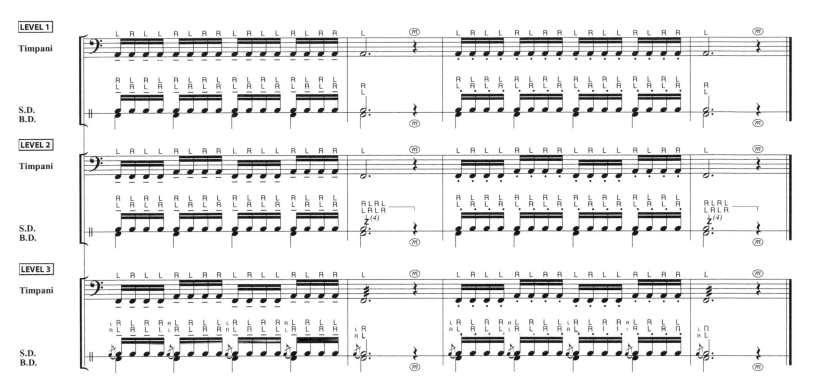

Percussion Goals

Level 1

1. Breathe together.
2. Start together.
3. **Match** articulation style of the wind players.
4. Release together.
5. Posture should be natural with the body position balanced. The body and face should remain still.
6. Use appropriate pedaling and dampening to match length of notes of the wind players.
7. Strike the instrument in the same place, with the same **energy** every time.
8. Hands, wrists and arms should look natural and feel soft and relaxed.
9. The notes should not weaken as rhythms become more active.
10. Breathe on count 4 quarter rests
11. All parts are interchangeable, but should remain in **balance** throughout.
12. Each note should not be louder or softer than the note preceding it.

Level 2/3

P	1.	All flams should have the same quality of sound.
P	2.	As rhythms become more active, they should not get louder or softer.
K,T	3.	As pitches ascend, the higher note should not be louder than the lower note.
K,T	4.	As pitches descend, the lower note should not be softer than the higher note.
P,K,T	5.	Rolls should be smooth and even, without extraneous noises.

5–9 Style Exercise – Minor Thirds/Non-Changing Notes

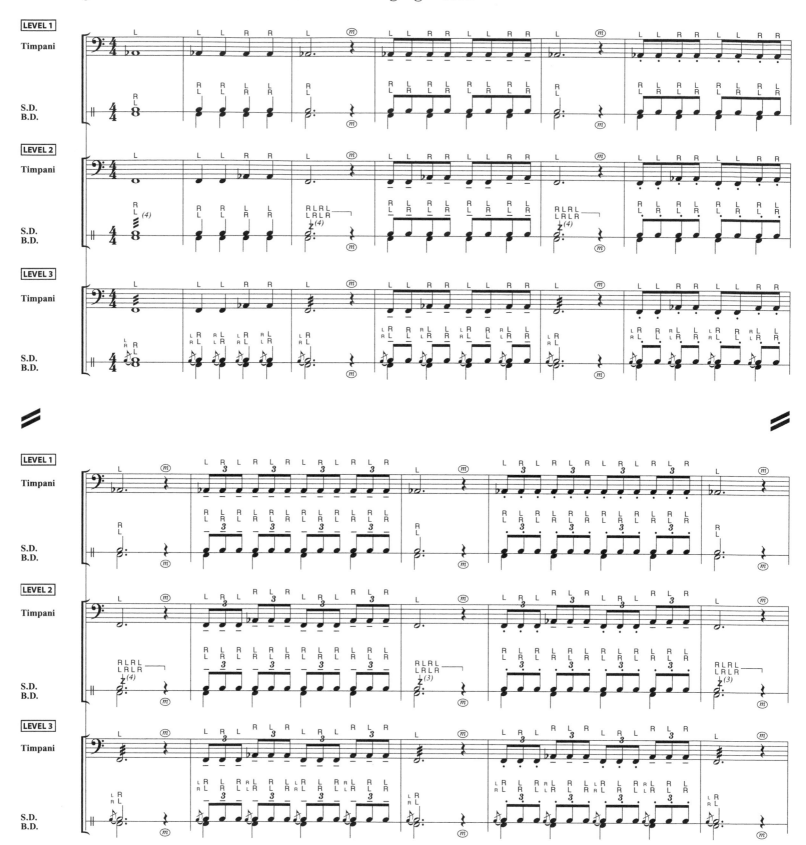

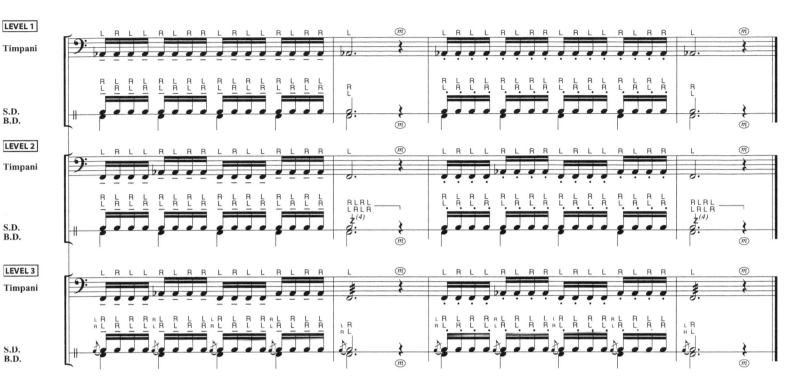

 ## Percussion Goals
Level 1
1. Breathe together.
2. Start together.
3. Strike the instrument in the same place, with the same **energy** every time.
4. **Match** the articulation style of the wind players.
5. Posture should be natural with the body position balanced. The body and face should remain still.
6. The stroke beginnings and ends should be smooth (touch-lift strokes).
7. Hands, wrists and arms should look natural and feel soft and relaxed.
8. The quicker the notes, the smoother the mallets/sticks should look. The mallets/sticks should move WITH the hands, NOT as a reaction to that movement.
9. Breathe on count 4 quarter rests.
10. All parts are interchangeable, but should remain in **balance** throughout.
11. As pitches ascend, the higher note should not be louder than the lower note.
12. As pitches descend, the lower note should not be softer than the higher note.

K,T 13. When applicable, use appropriate pedaling and dampening to **match** the articulation length of the wind players.

Level 2/3
P 1. All flams should have the same quality of sound.

K,T 2. Do not accent the beginnings of rolls.

P,K,T 3. Rolls should be smooth and even, without extraneous noises.

5–10 Style Exercise – Major Seconds/Non-Changing Notes

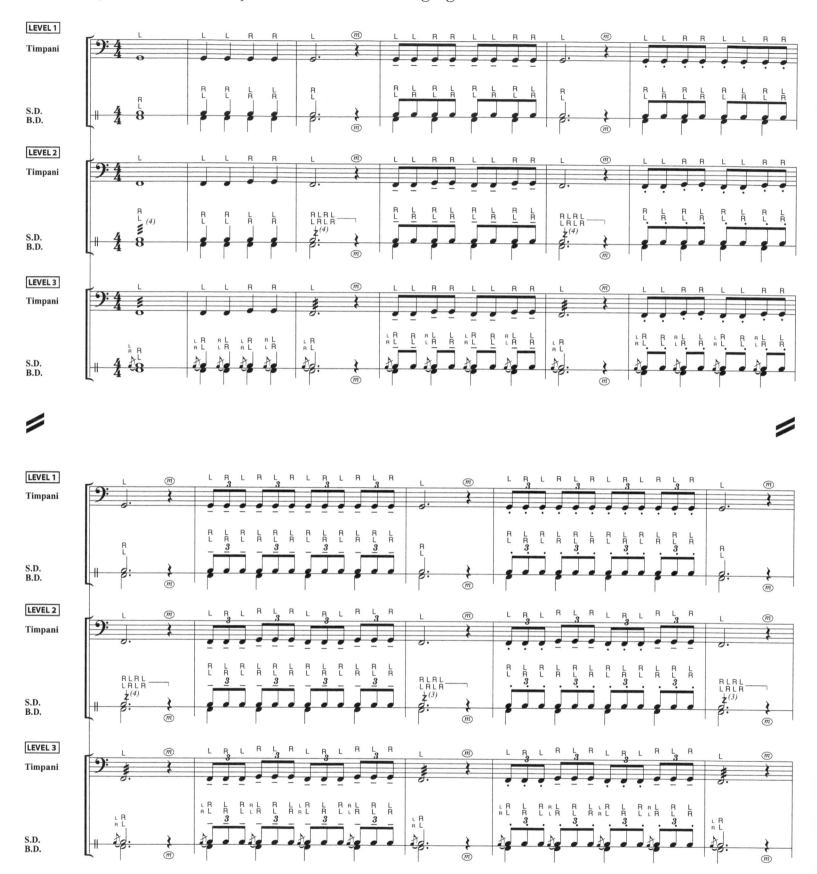

 ## Percussion Goals

Level 1

1. Breathe together.
2. Start together.
3. Strike the instrument in the same place, with the same **energy** every time.
4. **Match** the articulation style of the wind players.
5. Posture should be natural with the body position balanced. The body and face should remain still.
6. The stroke beginnings and ends should be smooth (touch-lift strokes).
7. Hands, wrists and arms should look natural and feel soft and relaxed.
8. The quicker the notes, the smoother the mallets/sticks should look. The mallets/sticks should move WITH the hands, NOT as a reaction to that movement.
9. Breathe on count 4 quarter rests.
10. All parts are interchangeable, but should remain in **balance** throughout.
11. As pitches ascend, the higher note should not be louder than the lower note.
12. As pitches descend, the lower note should not be softer than the higher note.

K,T 13. When applicable, use appropriate pedaling and dampening to **match** the articulation length of the wind players.

Level 2/3

P 1. All flams should have the same quality of sound.

K,T 2. Do not accent the beginnings of rolls.

P,K,T 3. Rolls should be smooth and even, without extraneous noises.

5–11 Style Exercise – Perfect Fifths/Non-Changing Notes

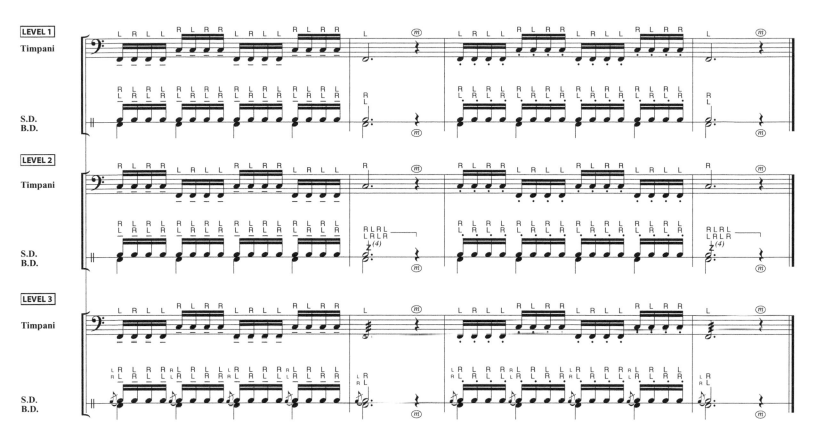

 ## Percussion Goals

Level 1

1. Breathe together.
2. Start together.
3. Strike the instrument in the same place, with the same energy every time.
4. **Match** the articulation style of the wind players.
5. Posture should be natural with the body position balanced. The body and face should remain still.
6. The stroke beginnings and ends should be smooth (touch-lift strokes).
7. Hands, wrists and arms should look natural and feel soft and relaxed.
8. The quicker the notes, the smoother the mallets/sticks should look. The mallets/sticks should move WITH the hands, NOT as a reaction to that movement.
9. Breathe on count 4 quarter rests.
10. As pitches ascend, the higher note should not be louder than the lower note.
11. As pitches descend, the lower note should not be softer than the higher note.

K,T 12. When applicable, use appropriate pedaling and dampening to **match** the articulation length of the wind players.

Level 2/3

P 1. All flams should have the same quality of sound.

K,T 2. Do not accent the beginnings of rolls.

P,K,T 3. Rolls should be smooth and even, without extraneous noises.

5–12 Style Exercise – Perfect Fourths/Changing Notes

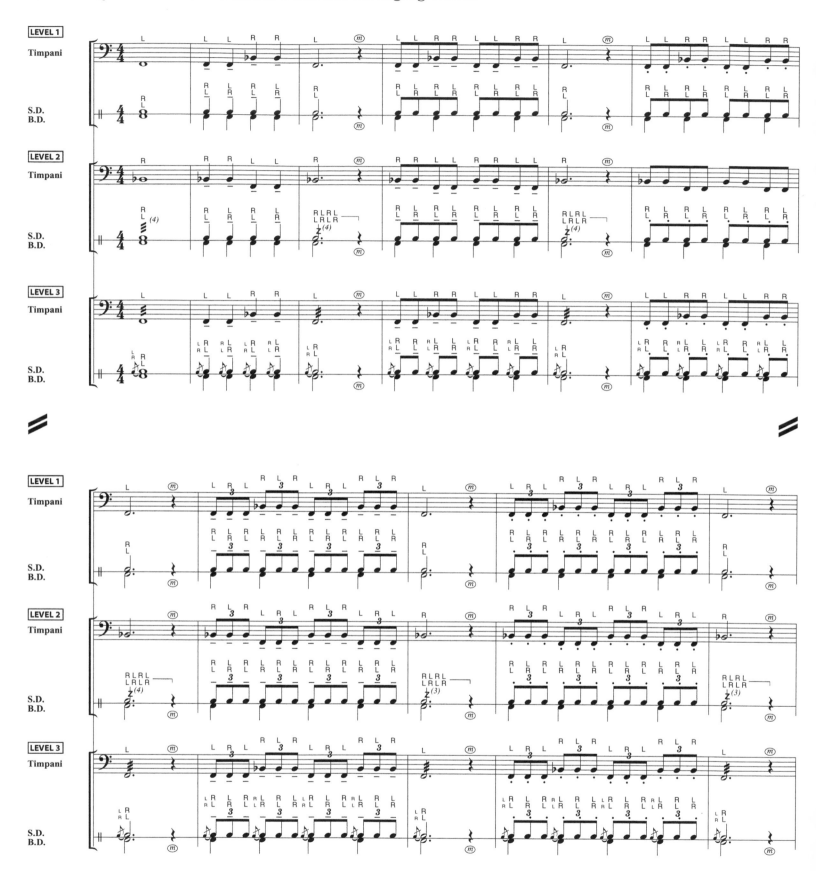

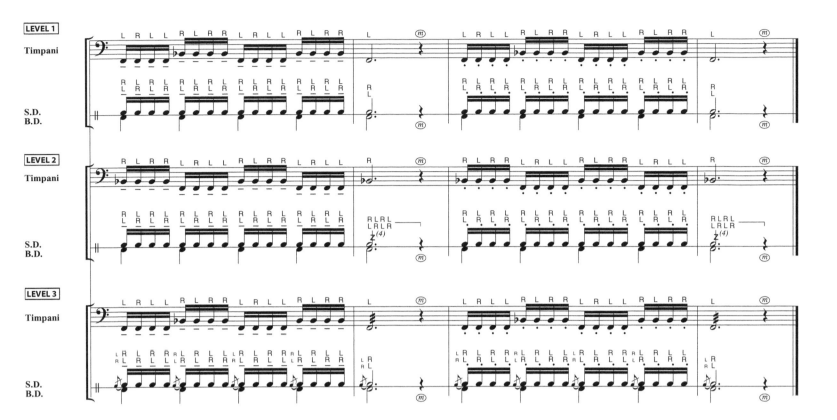

 Percussion Goals

Level 1

1. Breathe together.
2. Start together.
3. Strike the instrument in the same place, with the same **energy** every time.
4. **Match** the articulation style of the wind players.
5. Posture should be natural with the body position balanced. The body and face should remain still.
6. The stroke beginnings and ends should be smooth (touch-lift strokes).
7. Hands, wrists and arms should look natural and feel soft and relaxed.
8. The quicker the notes, the smoother the mallets/sticks should look. The mallets/sticks should move WITH the hands, NOT as a reaction to that movement.
9. Breathe on count 4 quarter rests.
10. As pitches ascend, the higher note should not be louder than the lower note.
11. As pitches descend, the lower note should not be softer than the higher note.

K,T 12. When applicable, use appropriate pedaling and dampening to match the articulation length of the wind players.

Level 2/3

P 1. All flams should have the same quality of sound.

K,T 2. Do not accent the beginnings of rolls.

P,K,T 3. Rolls should be smooth and even, without extraneous noises.

5–13 Style Exercise – Major Thirds/Changing Notes

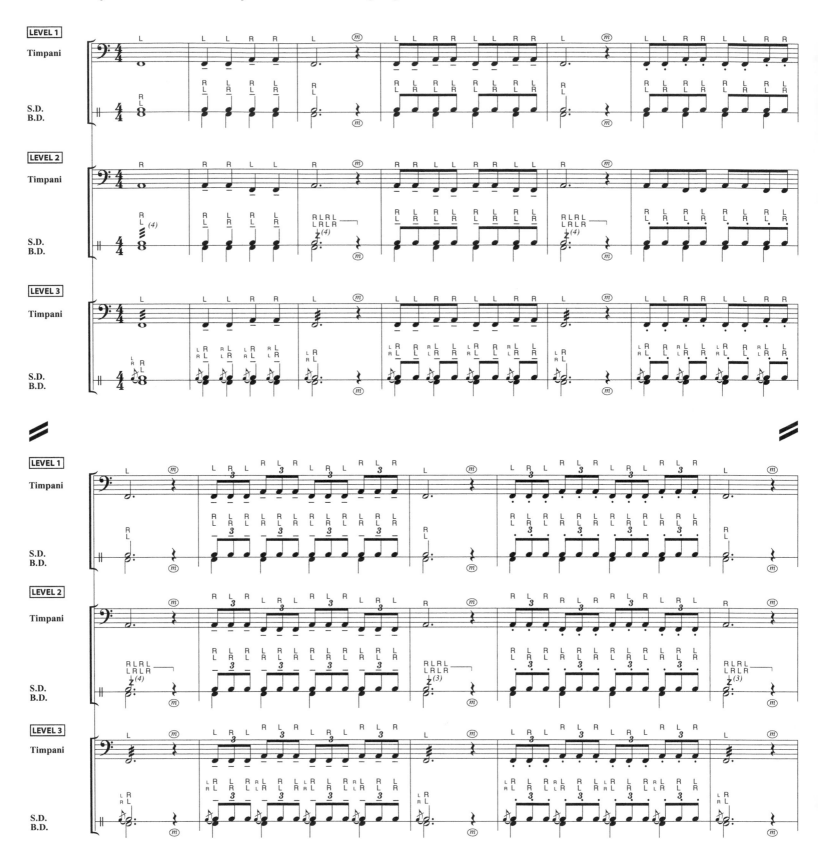

 Percussion Goals

Level 1
1. Breathe together.
2. Start together.
3. Strike the instrument in the same place, with the same **energy** every time.
4. **Match** the articulation style of the wind players.
5. Posture should be natural with the body position balanced. The body and face should remain still.
6. The stroke beginnings and ends should be smooth (touch-lift strokes).
7. Hands, wrists and arms should look natural and feel soft and relaxed.
8. The quicker the notes, the smoother the mallets/sticks should look. The mallets/sticks should move WITH the hands, NOT as a reaction to that movement.
9. Breathe on count 4 quarter rests.
10. As pitches ascend, the higher note should not be louder than the lower note.
11. As pitches descend, the lower note should not be softer than the higher note.

K,T 12. When applicable, use appropriate pedaling and dampening to match the articulation length of the wind players.

Level 2/3
P 1. All flams should have the same quality of sound.
K,T 2. Do not accent the beginnings of rolls.
P,K,T 3. Rolls should be smooth and even, without extraneous noises.

5-14 Style Exercise – Minor Thirds/Changing Notes

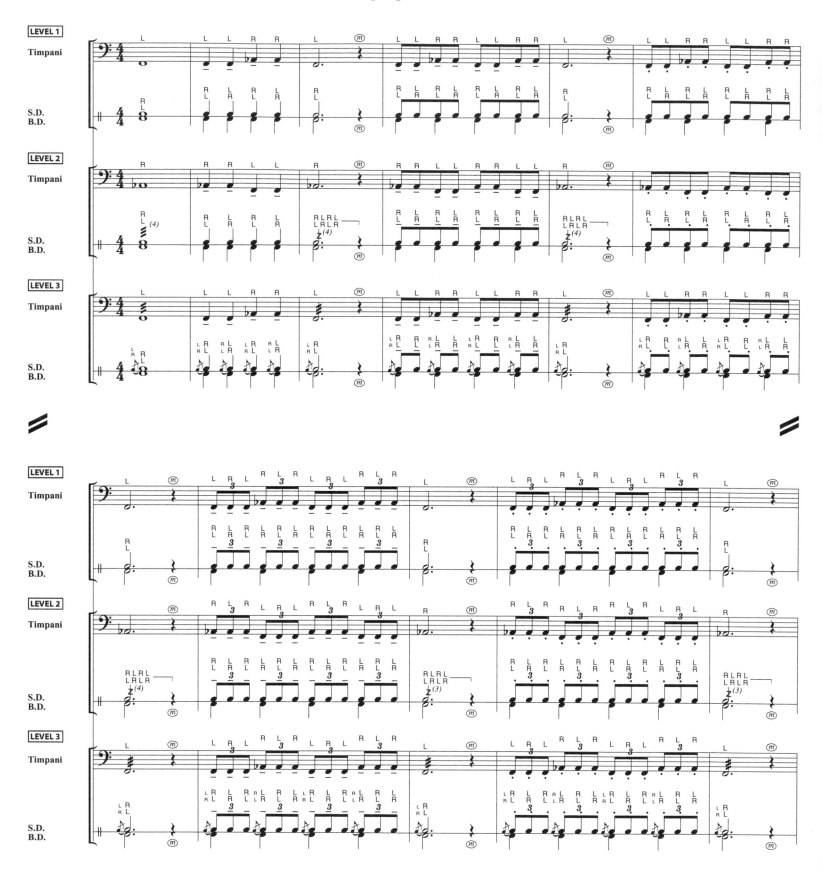

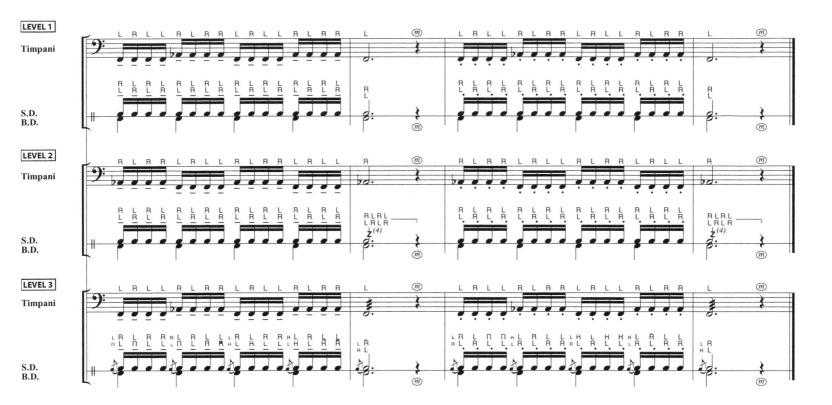

 Percussion Goals

Level 1

1. Breathe together.
2. Start together.
3. Strike the instrument in the same place, with the same **energy** every time.
4. **Match** the articulation style of the wind players.
5. Posture should be natural with the body position balanced. The body and face should remain still.
6. The stroke beginnings and ends should be smooth (touch-lift strokes).
7. Hands, wrists and arms should look natural and feel soft and relaxed.
8. The quicker the notes, the smoother the mallets/sticks should look. The mallets/sticks should move WITH the hands, NOT as a reaction to that movement.
9. Breathe on count 4 quarter rests.
10. As pitches ascend, the higher note should not be louder than the lower note.
11. As pitches descend, the lower note should not be softer than the higher note.

K,T 12. When applicable, use appropriate pedaling and dampening to match the articulation length of the wind players.

Level 2/3

P   1. All flams should have the same quality of sound.
K,T   2. Do not accent the beginnings of rolls.
P,K,T 3. Rolls should be smooth and even, without extraneous noises.

5–15 Style Exercise – Major Seconds/Changing Notes

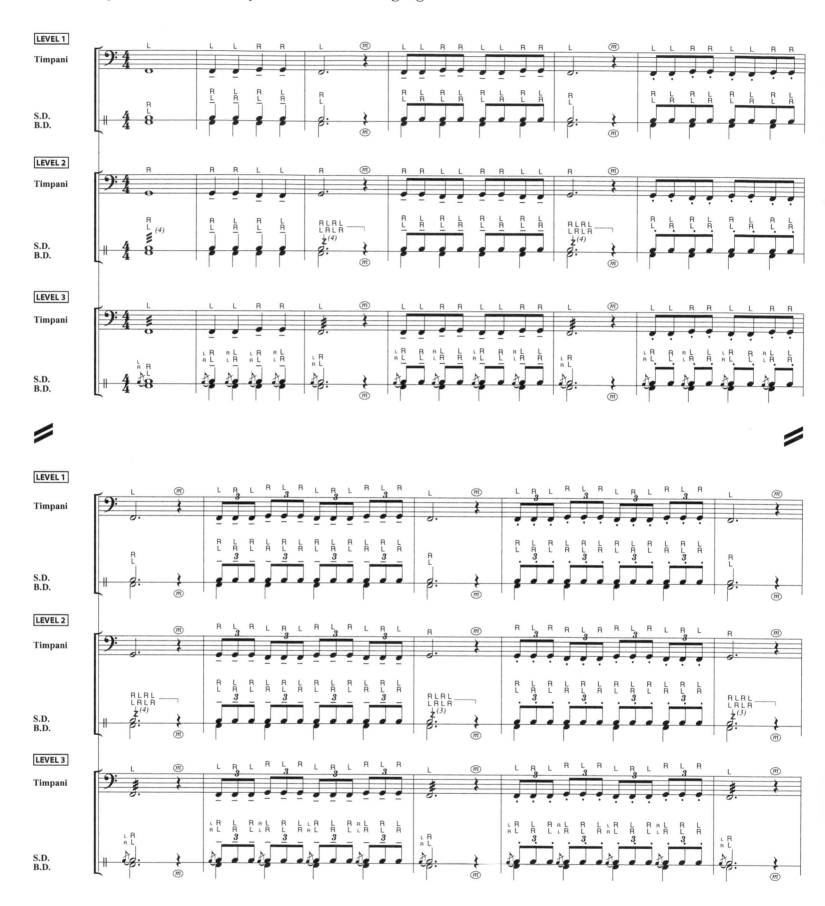

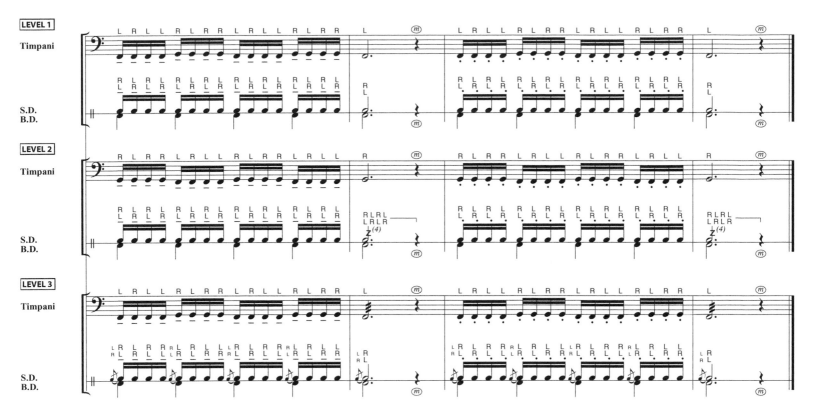

Percussion Goals

Level 1
1. Breathe together.
2. Start together.
3. Strike the instrument in the same place, with the same **energy** every time.
4. **Match** the articulation style of the wind players.
5. Posture should be natural with the body position balanced. The body and face should remain still.
6. The stroke beginnings and ends should be smooth (touch-lift strokes).
7. Hands, wrists and arms should look natural and feel soft and relaxed.
8. The quicker the notes, the smoother the mallets/sticks should look. The mallets/sticks should move WITH the hands, NOT as a reaction to that movement.
9. Breathe on count 4 quarter rests.
10. As pitches ascend, the higher note should not be louder than the lower note.
11. As pitches descend, the lower note should not be softer than the higher note.

K,T 12. When applicable, use appropriate pedaling and dampening to match the articulation length of the wind players.

Level 2/3
P 1. All flams should have the same quality of sound.

K,T 2. Do not accent the beginnings of rolls.

P,K,T 3. Rolls should be smooth and even, without extraneous noises.

6. Creating Intervals with a Pedal Tone

6–1 Ascending Intervals With Pedal Tone

Percussion Goals

Level 1

1. Breathe together.
2. Start together.
3. Release together.
4. **Match** the line tonally, with the same **energy**/dynamic level
5. Rolls should be smooth and even, without extraneous noise.
6. **Organize** the end of each note as clearly as the beginning.
7. Where applicable, dampen to match the ends of the wind players' notes.
8. The hand, wrist and arm motion should look the same hand-to-hand.
9. Line A – breathe on count 4 quarter rests.

P   10. Snare drum roll speed (16th note, 8th note, 16th note triplet base) should be determined by the tempo.

A   11. Triangle and tambourine: each should have a consistent quality of sound, note-to-note.

Level 2/3

A   1. The suspended cymbal roll should be smooth and even, without extraneous noise.

K,T   2. When playing the two note rolls, the ascending interval should not be stronger than the **pedal tone**.

Boldface words are terms that can be found in the glossary at the back of the book.

Goal Key: **P**=Snare, Bass Drum and Cymbals; **K**=Keyboard; **A**=Auxiliary; **T**=Timpani

ⓜ = Muffle (dampen)

6–2 Descending Intervals With Pedal Tone

Percussion Goals
Level 1
1. Breathe together.
2. Start together.
3. Release together.
4. **Match** the line tonally, with the same **energy**/dynamic level
5. Rolls should be smooth and even, without extraneous noise.
6. **Organize** the end of each note as clearly as the beginning.
7. Where applicable, dampen to match the ends of the wind players' notes.
8. The hand, wrist and arm motion should look the same hand-to-hand.
9. Line A – breathe on count 4 quarter rests.

P 10. Snare drum roll speed (16th note, 8th note, 16th note triplet base) should be determined by the tempo.

A 11. Triangle and tambourine: each should have a consistent quality of sound, note-to-note.

Level 2/3
P 1. Rolls should be smooth and even, without extraneous noise.

K,T 2. When playing the two note rolls, the descending interval should maintain the same **tonal energy** as the **pedal tone**.

6–3 Parallel Intervals With Pedal Tone

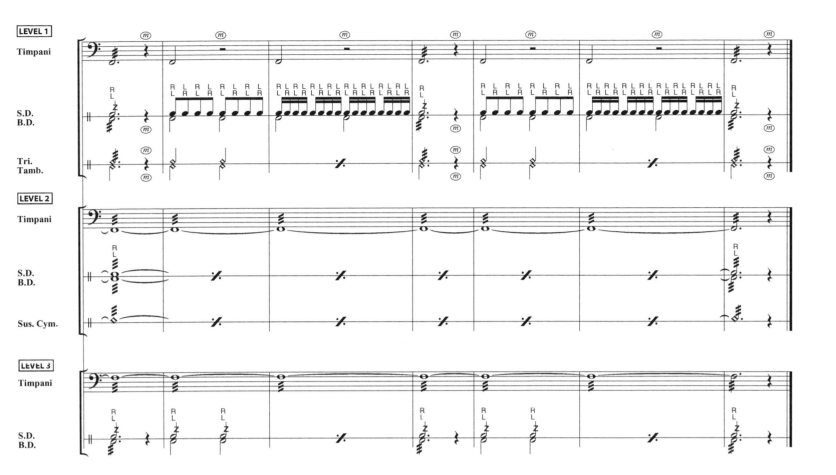

 ## Percussion Goals

Level 1

1. Breathe together.
2. Start together.
3. Release together.
4. Line A note beginnings should **match** dynamically regardless of interval.
5. Line A – breathe on count 4 quarter rests.

A 6. Triangle and tambourine: each should have a consistent quality of sound, note-to-note.

Level 2/3

P 1. Rolls should be smooth and even, without extraneous noise.

K 2. Notes played in octaves should sound at exactly the same time; subdivide internally.

K 3. When playing the two note rolls, the moving note should not be stronger or weaker than the **pedal tone**.

6–4 Interval Pass-through

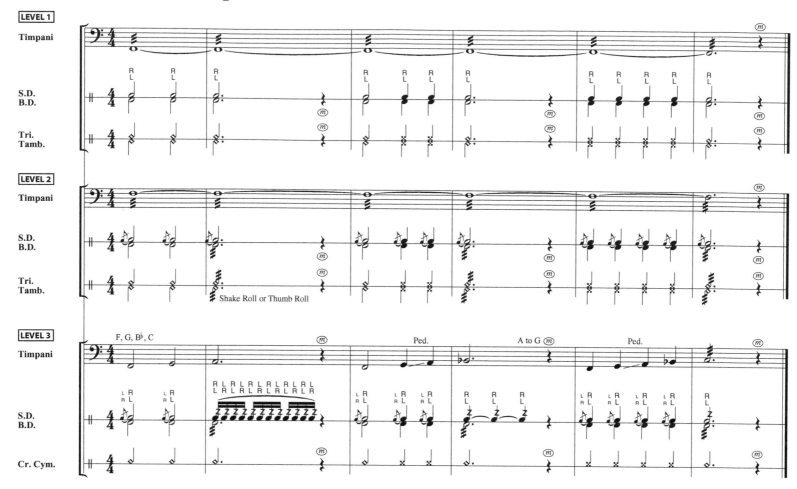

 Percussion Goals

Level 1

1. Breathe together.
2. Start together.
3. Release together.
4. **Match** the group tonally, with the same **energy**/dynamic level.
5. Line A – at the beginning, the second note leads the line forward and functions as part of the cadence, so it should lead strongly from the first note but be equal to the third note. Do the same for measures 3-4 and 5-6.
6. Rolls should be smooth and even, without extraneous noise.
7. Line A – breathe on count 4 quarter rests.

A 8. Triangle and tambourine: each should have a consistent quality of sound, note-to-note.

Level 2/3

P 1. All flams should have the same quality of sound throughout.
P 2. Rolls should be smooth and even, without extraneous noise.
K 3. Notes played in octaves should sound at exactly the same time; subdivide internally.
K 4. When playing the two note rolls, the moving note should not be stronger or weaker than the **pedal tone**.

This page intentionally left blank to facilitate page turn.

6–5 Combined Perfect Fifths With Pedal Tone

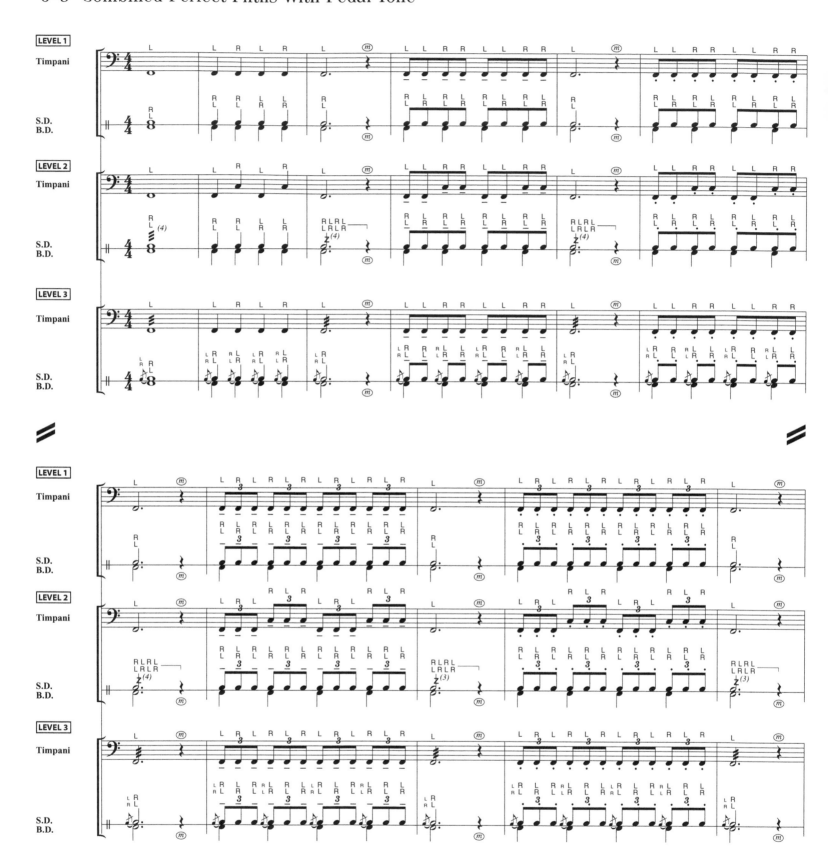

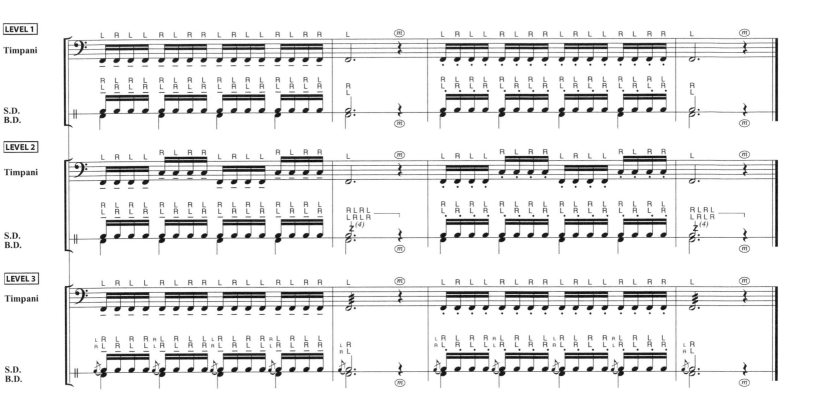

Percussion Goals
Level 1
1. Breathe together.
2. Start together.
3. Strike the instrument in the same place, with the same **energy** every time.
4. **Match** the articulation style of the wind players.
5. Posture should be natural with the body position balanced. The body and face should remain still.
6. The stroke beginnings and ends should be smooth (touch-lift strokes).
7. Hands, wrists and arms should look natural and feel soft and relaxed.
8. The quicker the notes, the smoother the mallets/sticks should look. The mallets/sticks should move WITH the hands, NOT as a reaction to that movement.
9. Breathe on count 4 quarter rests..
10. As pitches ascend, the higher note should not be louder than the lower note.
11. As pitches descend, the lower note should not be softer than the higher note.
12. The **pedal tone** should match the **tonal energy**/dynamic level of the changing notes.
K,T 13. When applicable, use appropriate pedaling and dampening to match the articulation length of the wind players.
Level 2/3
P 1. All flams should have the same quality of sound.
K,T 2. Do not accent the beginnings of rolls.
P,K,T 3. Rolls should be smooth and even, without extraneous noises.

6-6 Combined Perfect Fourths With Pedal Tone

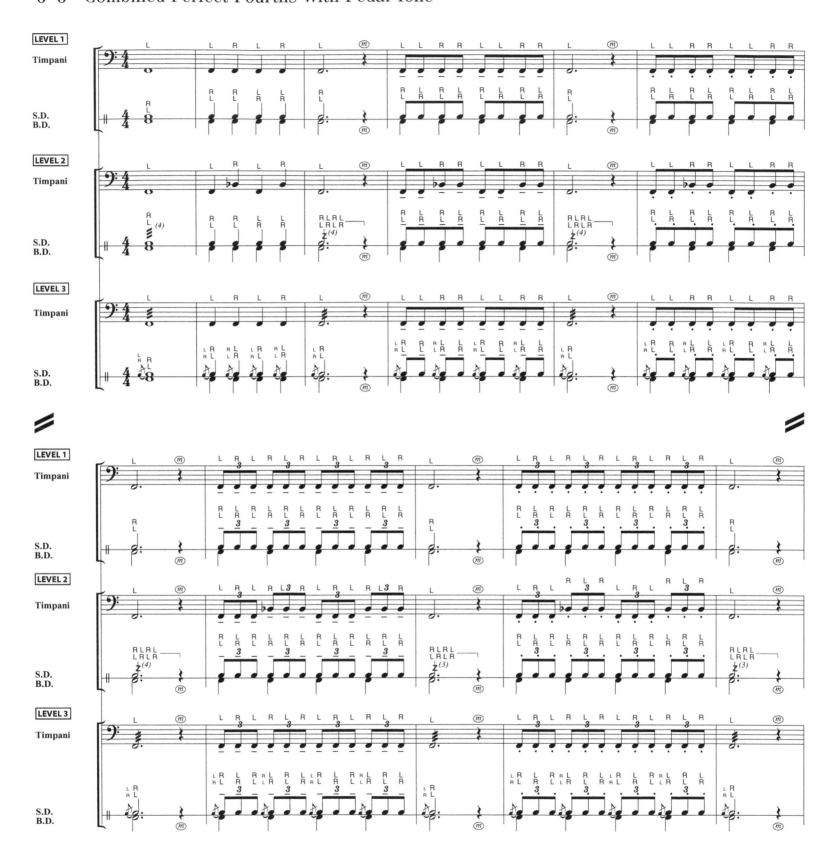

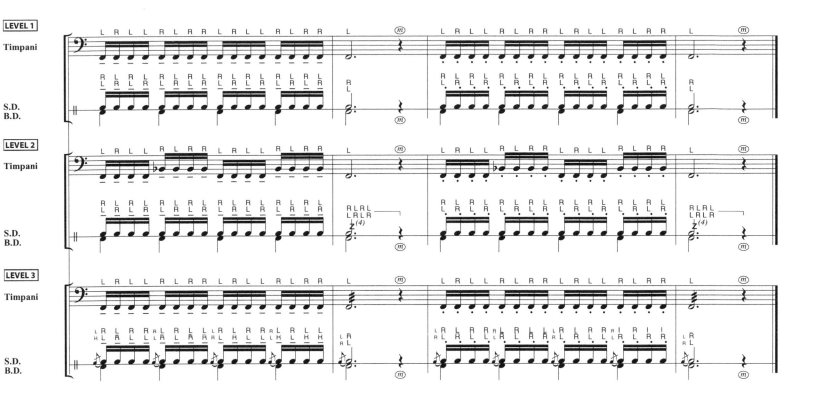

Percussion Goals

Level 1

1. Breathe together.
2. Start together.
3. Strike the instrument in the same place, with the same **energy** every time.
4. **Match** the articulation style of the wind players.
5. Posture should be natural with the body position balanced. The body and face should remain still.
6. The stroke beginnings and ends should be smooth (touch-lift strokes).
7. Hands, wrists and arms should look natural and feel soft and relaxed.
8. The quicker the notes, the smoother the mallets/sticks should look. The mallets/sticks should move WITH the hands, NOT as a reaction to that movement.
9. Breathe on count 4 quarter rests..
10. As pitches ascend, the higher note should not be louder than the lower note.
11. As pitches descend, the lower note should not be softer than the higher note.
12. The **pedal tone** should match the **tonal energy**/dynamic level of the changing notes.

K,T 13. When applicable, use appropriate pedaling and dampening to match the articulation length of the wind players.

Level 2/3

P 1. All flams should have the same quality of sound.

K,T 2. Do not accent the beginnings of rolls.

P,K,T 3. Rolls should be smooth and even, without extraneous noises.

6–7 Combined Major Thirds With Pedal Tone

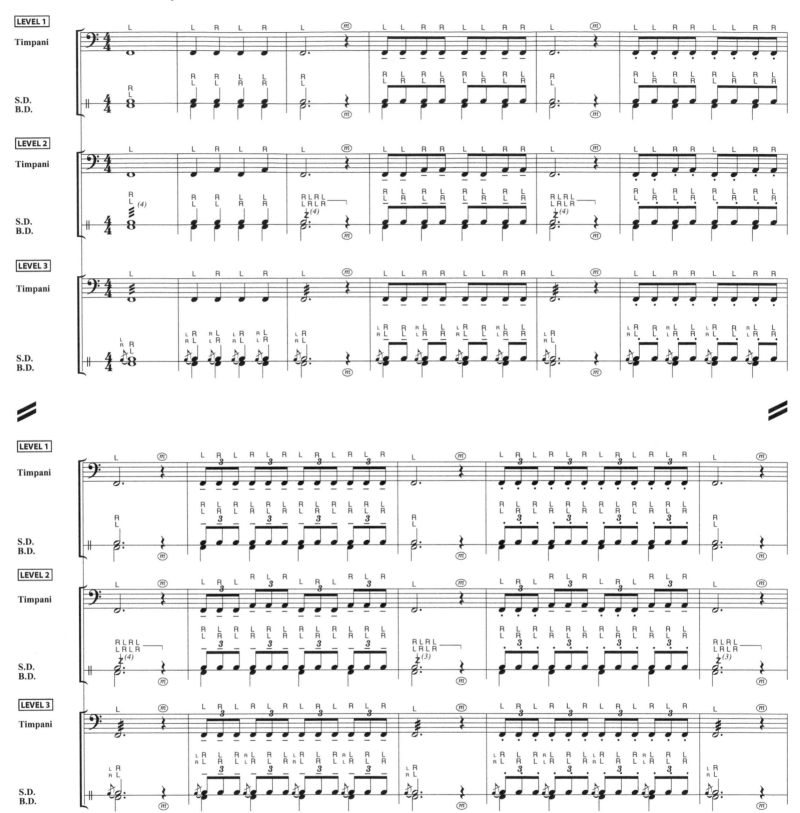

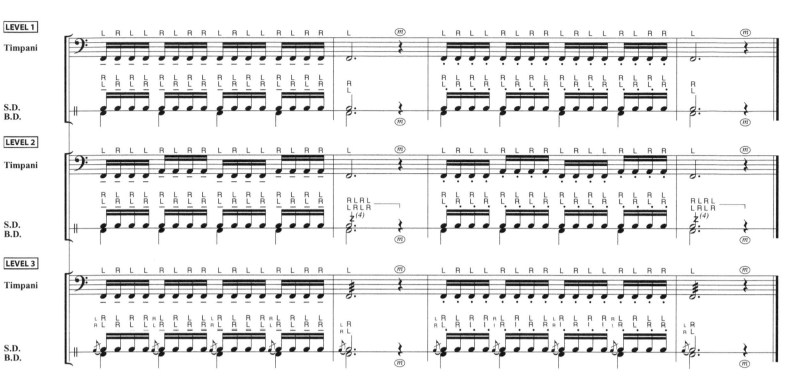

 ## Percussion Goals

Level 1

1. Breathe together.
2. Start together.
3. Strike the instrument in the same place, with the same **energy** every time.
4. **Match** the articulation style of the wind players.
5. Posture should be natural with the body position balanced. The body and face should remain still.
6. The stroke beginnings and ends should be smooth (touch-lift strokes).
7. Hands, wrists and arms should look natural and feel soft and relaxed.
8. The quicker the notes, the smoother the mallets/sticks should look. The mallets/sticks should move WITH the hands, NOT as a reaction to that movement.
9. Breathe on count 4 quarter rests..
10. As pitches ascend, the higher note should not be louder than the lower note.
11. As pitches descend, the lower note should not be softer than the higher note.
12. The **pedal tone** should match the **tonal energy**/dynamic level of the changing notes.

K,T 13. When applicable, use appropriate pedaling and dampening to match the articulation length of the wind players.

Level 2/3

P 1. All flams should have the same quality of sound.

K,T 2. Do not accent the beginnings of rolls.

P,K,T 4. Rolls should be smooth and even, without extraneous noises.

6–8 Combined Minor Thirds With Pedal Tone

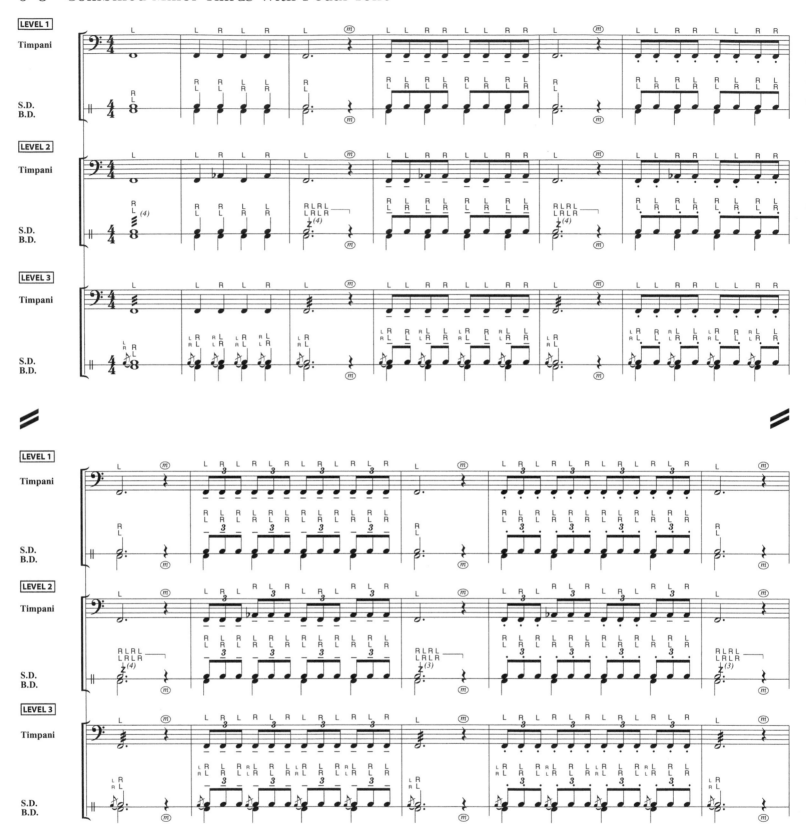

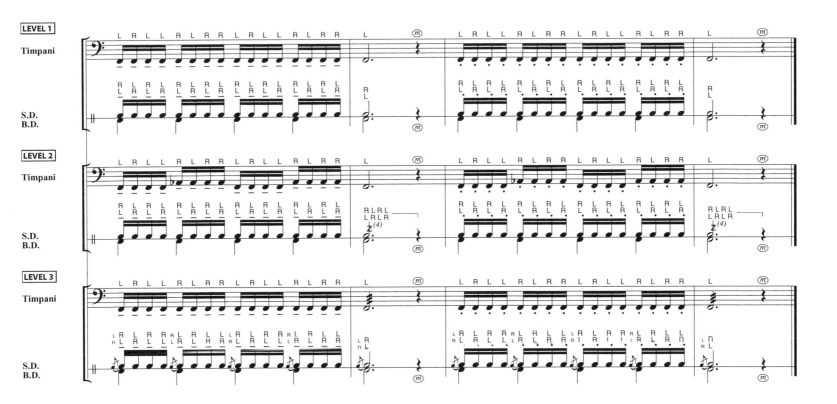

Percussion Goals

Level 1

1. Breathe together.
2. Start together.
3. Strike the instrument in the same place, with the same **energy** every time.
4. **Match** the articulation style of the wind players.
5. Posture should be natural with the body position balanced. The body and face should remain still.
6. The stroke beginnings and ends should be smooth (touch-lift strokes).
7. Hands, wrists and arms should look natural and feel soft and relaxed.
8. The quicker the notes, the smoother the mallets/sticks should look. The mallets/sticks should move WITH the hands, NOT as a reaction to that movement.
9. Breathe on count 4 quarter rests..
10. As pitches ascend, the higher note should not be louder than the lower note.
11. As pitches descend, the lower note should not be softer than the higher note.
12. The **pedal tone** should match the **tonal energy**/dynamic level of the changing notes.
K,T 13. When applicable, use appropriate pedaling and dampening to match the articulation length of the wind players.

Level 2/3

P 1. All flams should have the same quality of sound.
K,T 2. Do not accent the beginnings of rolls.
P,K,T 3. Rolls should be smooth and even, without extraneous noises.

6–9 Combined Major Seconds With Pedal Tone

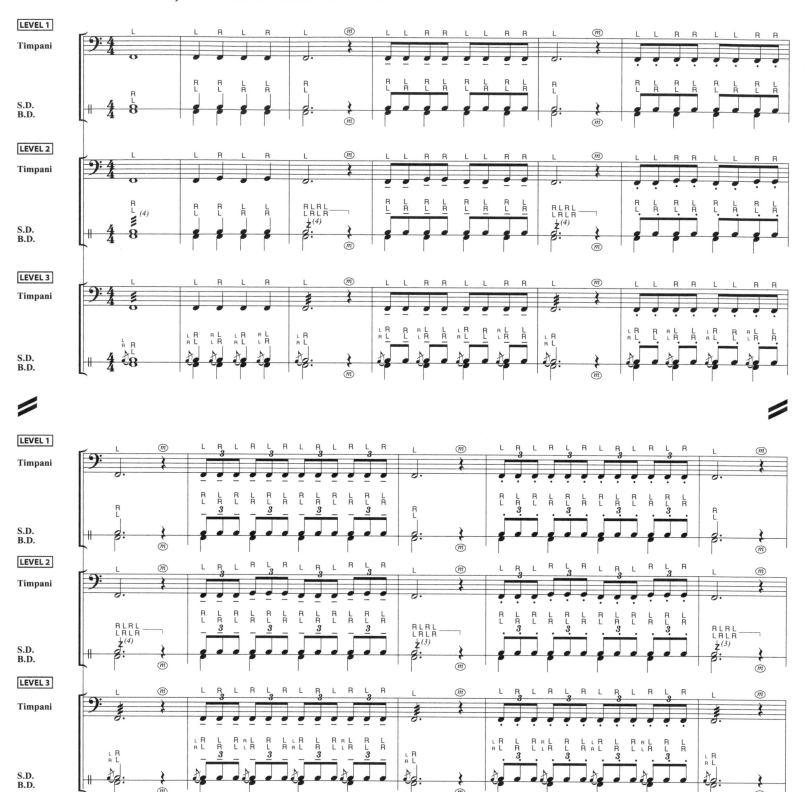

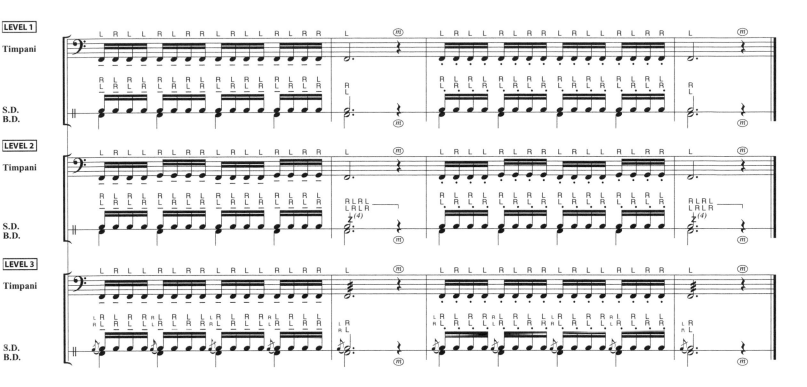

 ## Percussion Goals

Level 1
1. Breathe together.
2. Start together.
3. Strike the instrument in the same place, with the same **energy** every time.
4. **Match** the articulation style of the wind players.
5. Posture should be natural with the body position balanced. The body and face should remain still.
6. The stroke beginnings and ends should be smooth (touch-lift strokes).
7. Hands, wrists and arms should look natural and feel soft and relaxed.
8. The quicker the notes, the smoother the mallets/sticks should look. The mallets/sticks should move WITH the hands, NOT as a reaction to that movement.
9. Breathe on count 4 quarter rests..
10. As pitches ascend, the higher note should not be louder than the lower note.
11. As pitches descend, the lower note should not be softer than the higher note.
12. The **pedal tone** should match the **tonal energy**/dynamic level of the changing notes.

K,T 13. When applicable, use appropriate pedaling and dampening to match the articulation length of the wind players.
14. Don't back away from the whole step dissonance.

Level 2/3
P 1. All flams should have the same quality of sound.
K,T 2. Do not accent the beginnings of rolls.
P,K,T 3. Rolls should be smooth and even, without extraneous noises.

6–10 Combined Minor Seconds With Pedal Tone

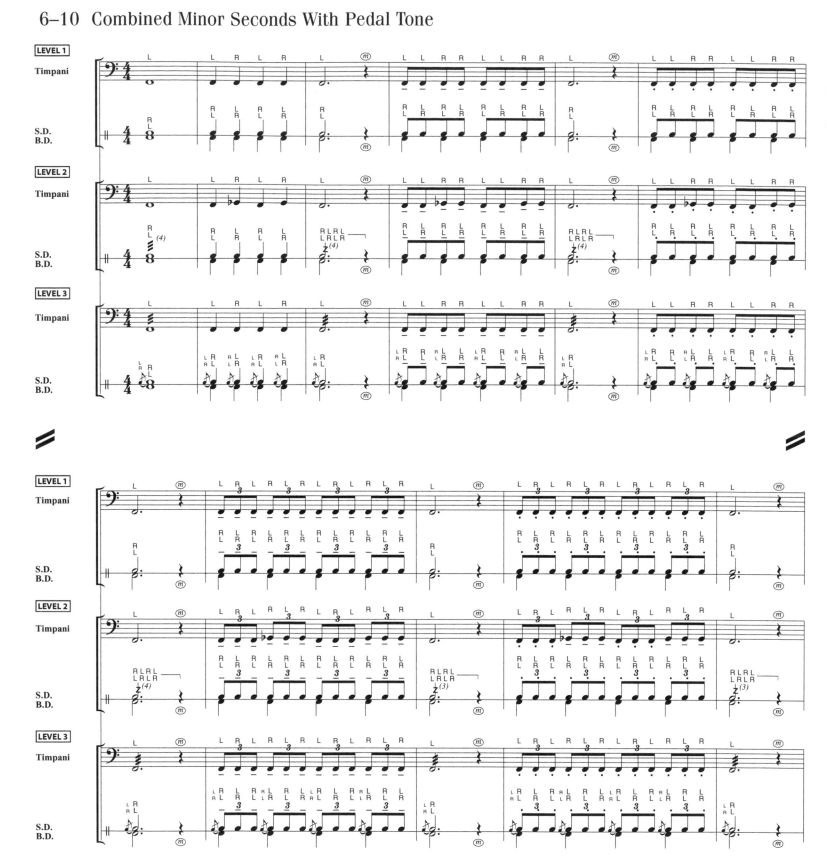

 Percussion Goals

Level 1

1. Breathe together.
2. Start together.
3. Strike the instrument in the same place, with the same **energy** every time.
4. **Match** the articulation style of the wind players.
5. Posture should be natural with the body position balanced. The body and face should remain still.
6. The stroke beginnings and ends should be smooth (touch-lift strokes).
7. Hands, wrists and arms should look natural and feel soft and relaxed.
8. The quicker the notes, the smoother the mallets/sticks should look. The mallets/sticks should move WITH the hands, NOT as a reaction to that movement.
9. Breathe on count 4 quarter rests..
10. As pitches ascend, the higher note should not be louder than the lower note.
11. As pitches descend, the lower note should not be softer than the higher note.
12. The **pedal tone** should match the **tonal energy**/dynamic level of the changing notes.
K,T 13. When applicable, use appropriate pedaling and dampening to match the articulation length of the wind players.
14. Don't back away from the whole step dissonance.

Level 2/3

P 1. All flams should have the same quality of sound.
K,T 2. Do not accent the beginnings of rolls.
P,K,T 3. Rolls should be smooth and even, without extraneous noises.

6–11 Small to Large Descending Intervals With Pedal Tone

Percussion Goals
Level 1
1. Breathe together.
2. Start together.
3. Strike the instrument in the same place, with the same energy every time.
4. Release together.
5. Rolls should be smooth and even, without extraneous noises.
6. **Balance** between parts should stay the same throughout.
7. **Match** the tonal **energy** of the wind players' note beginnings and endings.

Percussion Goals for Line A
P   1. All flams and ruffs should have the same quality of sound throughout.
A   2. Auxiliary percussion should produce the same **color** of sound every time.
T   3. While moving note-to-note, pedal action should be done quickly.
K,T   4. All parts are interchangeable, but should remain in balance throughout.

Percussion Goals for Line B
K,T   1. Do not accent the beginnings of rolls.
K,T   2. Breathe on count 3 during whole rests; breathe on count 4 quarter rests.

6–12 Small to Large Ascending Intervals With Pedal Tone

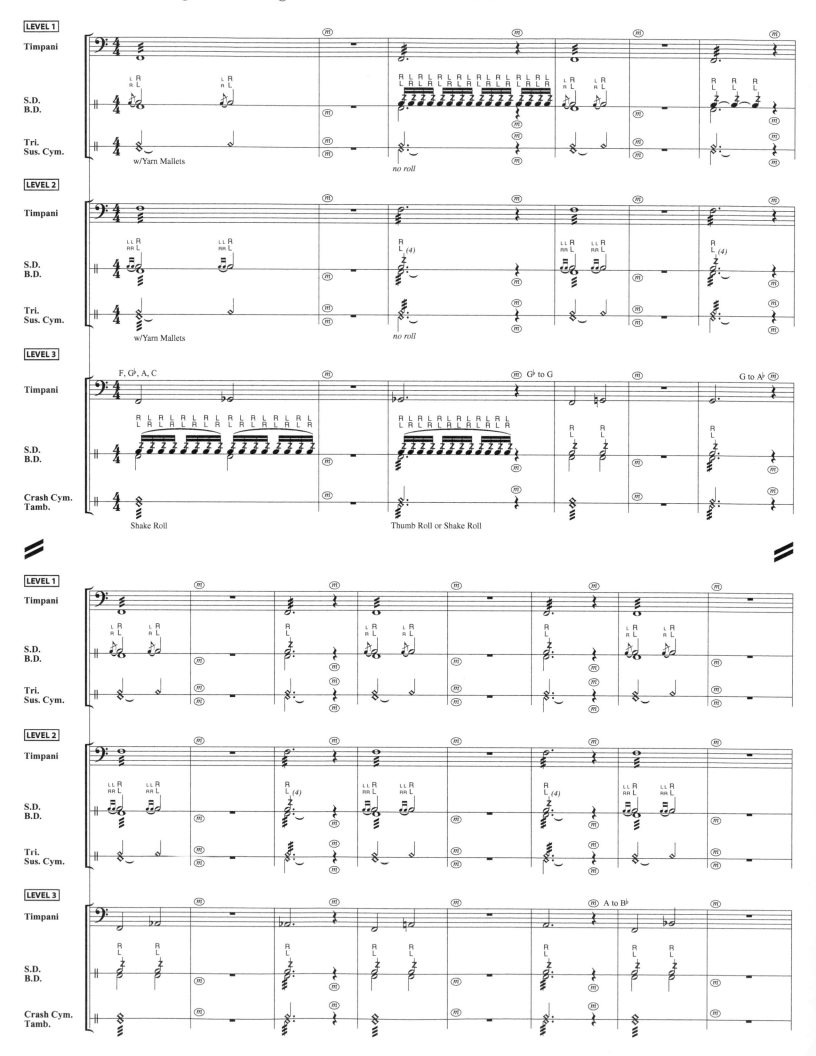

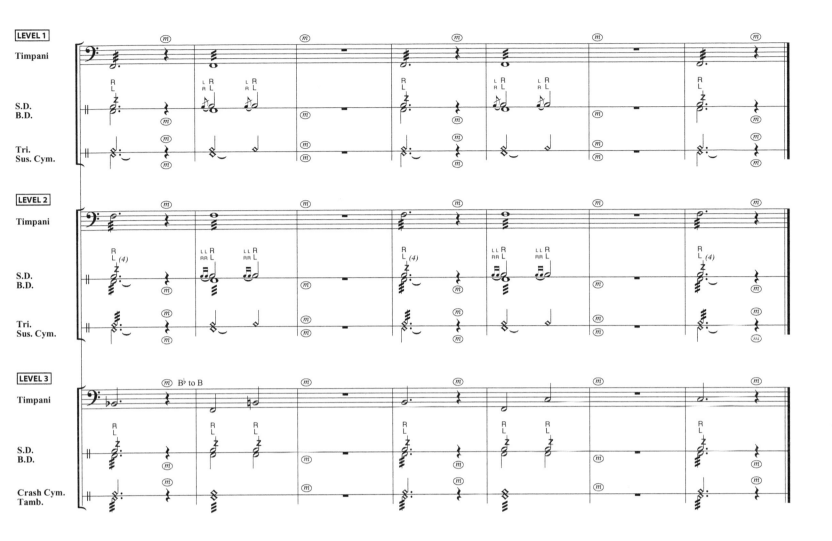

Percussion Goals (for 6–12, 6–13 and 6–14)

Level 1

1. Breathe together.
2. Start together.
3. Strike the instrument in the same place, with the same energy every time.
4. Release together.
5. Rolls should be smooth and even, without extraneous noises.
6. **Balance** between parts should stay the same throughout.
7. **Match** the tonal **energy** of the wind players' note beginnings and endings.

Percussion Goals for Line A (for 6–12, 6–13 and 6–14)

P   1. All flams and ruffs should have the same quality of sound throughout.
A   2. Auxiliary percussion should produce the same **color** of sound every time.
T   3. While moving note-to-note, pedal action should be done quickly.
K,T 4. All parts are interchangeable, but should remain in balance throughout.

Percussion Goals for Line B (for 6–12, 6–13 and 6–14)

K,T 1. Do not accent the beginnings of rolls.
K,T 2. Breathe on count 3 during whole rests; breathe on count 4 quarter rests.

6–13   Small to Large Descending Intervals With Pedal Tone

(Goals on p.93)

6–14 Small to Large Ascending Intervals With Pedal Tone
(Goals on p.93)

7. Extending Skills in Lower Register

7–1 Descending Concert F Scale (Two-Note Segments)

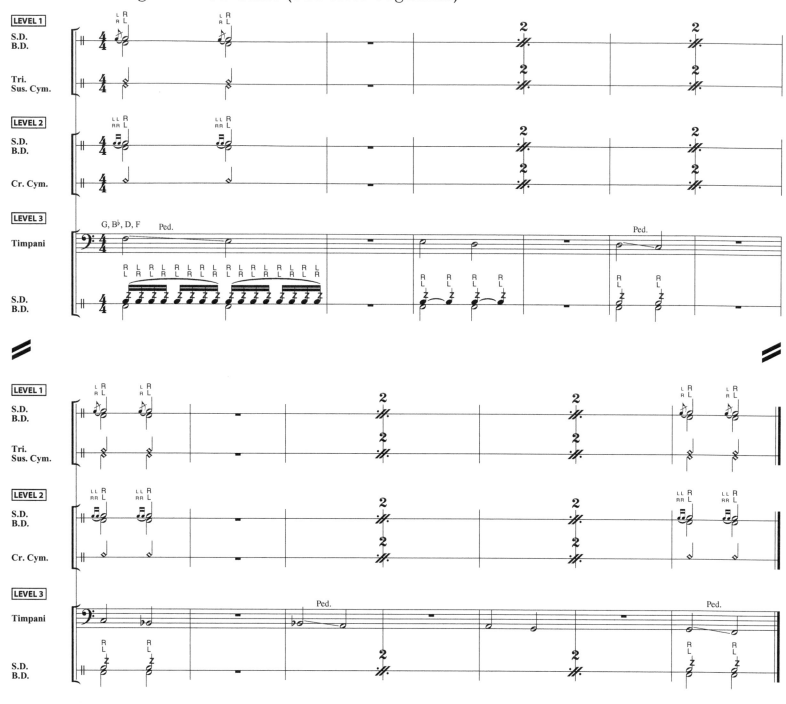

 Percussion Goals

Level 1

1. Breathe together.
2. Start together.
3. Strike the instrument in the same place, with the same **energy** every time.
4. Where applicable, dampen to **match** the ends of the wind players' notes.
- **A** 5. Auxiliary percussion should produce the same **color** of sound every time.

Level 2/3

- **P** 1. All flams and ruffs should have the same quality of sound throughout.
- **P** 2. Snare drum roll speed (16th note, 8th note, 16th note triplet base) should be determined by the tempo.
- **T** 3. Pedaling should occur (fast) just before the mallet strikes the head.
- **K,T** 4. The second note of any two-note pattern should be the same volume as the first.
- **K,T** 5. Do not accent the beginnings of rolls.
- **P,K,T** 6. Rolls should be smooth and even, without extraneous noise.

Boldface words are terms that can be found in the glossary at the back of the book.

Goal Key: **P**=Snare, Bass Drum and Cymbals; **K**=Keyboard; **A**=Auxiliary; **T**=Timpani

ⓜ = Muffle (dampen)

7–2 Descending Concert F Scale – WW Model/Brass Lip Vibrations (Four and Eight-Note Segments)

* Silently finger/position written notes while
remaining in correct playing position.

 Percussion Goals

Level 1
1. Breathe together.
2. Start together.
3. Strike the instrument in the same place, with the same **energy** every time.
4. Where applicable, dampen to **match** the ends of the wind players' notes.
5. This exercise can be practiced with single strokes or rolls.
6. Listen to make sure that the **balance** to the wind players remains constant.
A   7. Auxiliary percussion should produce the same **color** of sound every time.

Level 2/3
P   1. Snare drum roll speed (16th note, 8th note, 16th note triplet base) should be determined by the tempo.
K   2. Notes played in octaves should sound exactly together; subdivide internally.
T   3. Pedaling should occur (fast) just before the mallet strikes the head.
P,K,T 4. Rolls should be smooth and even, without extraneous noise.

7–3 Descending Concert F Scale – WW Model (Triple Rhythms)/Brass Half Notes (Four and Eight-Note Segments)

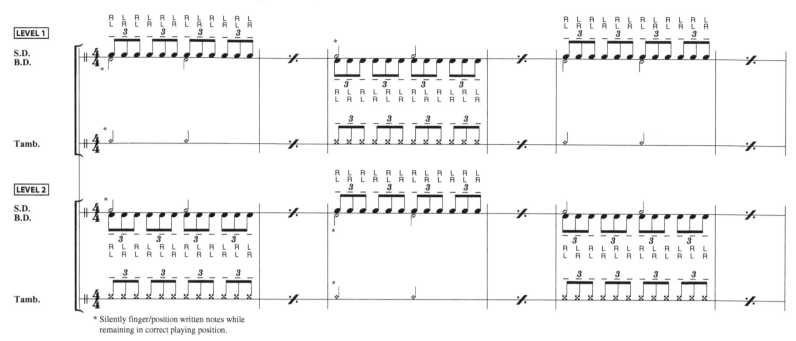

* Silently finger/position written notes while remaining in correct playing position.

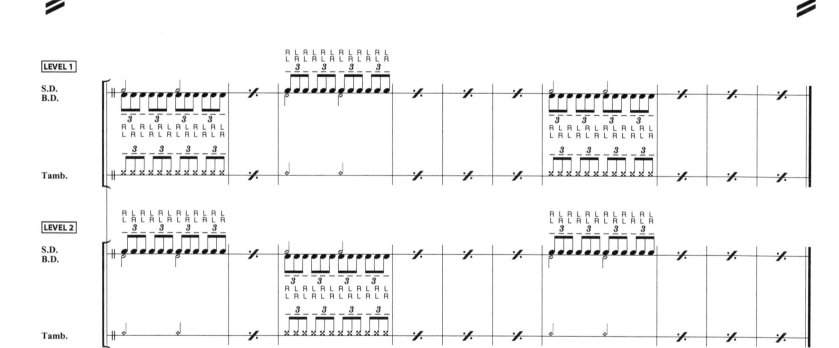

Percussion Goals

Level 1

1. Breathe together.
2. Start together.
3. Strike the instrument in the same place, with the same **energy** every time.
4. Where applicable, dampen to **match** the ends of the wind players' notes.
5. Match the articulation style/dynamic level of the wind players.
6. Breathe on count 3 before entrances
7. This exercise can be practiced with single strokes or rolls.
8. Listen to make sure that the **balance** to the wind players remains constant.

A 9. Auxiliary percussion should produce the same **color** of sound every time.

Level 2

P,K,T 1. Hand, wrist and arm movement should be smooth and fluid.

7–4 Complete Descending Concert F Scale – WW Model/Brass Lip Vibrations (Two-Note Segments)

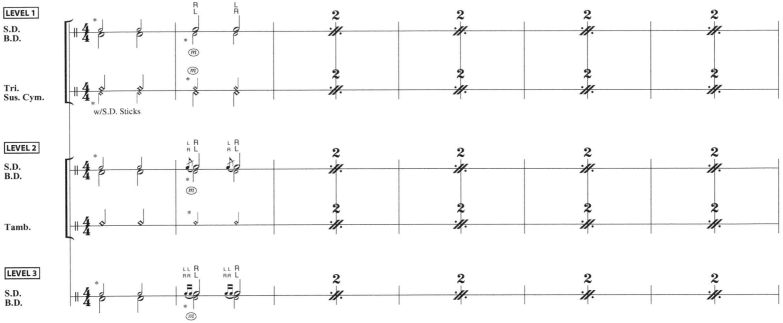

* Silently finger/position written notes while
  remaining in correct playing position.

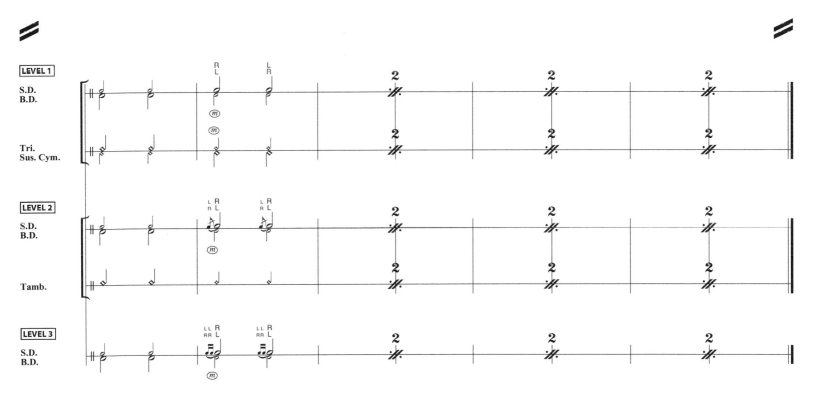

 ## Percussion Goals

Level 1
1. Breathe together.
2. Start together.
3. Strike the instrument in the same place, with the same **energy** every time.
4. Where applicable, dampen to **match** the ends of the wind players' notes.
5. Match the articulation style/dynamic level of the wind players.
6. Breathe on count 3 before entrances
7. This exercise can be practiced with single strokes or rolls.
8. Listen to make sure that the **balance** to the wind players remains constant.
A   9. Auxiliary percussion should produce the same **color** of sound every time.

Level 2/3
P   1. All flams and ruffs should have the same quality of sound throughout.
K   2. Notes played in octaves should sound at exactly the same time; subdivide internally.
K,T 3. Rolls should be smooth and even, without extraneous noise.

7–5 Complete Descending Concert F Scale – WW Model (Duple Rhythms)/Brass Half Notes (Two-Note Segments)

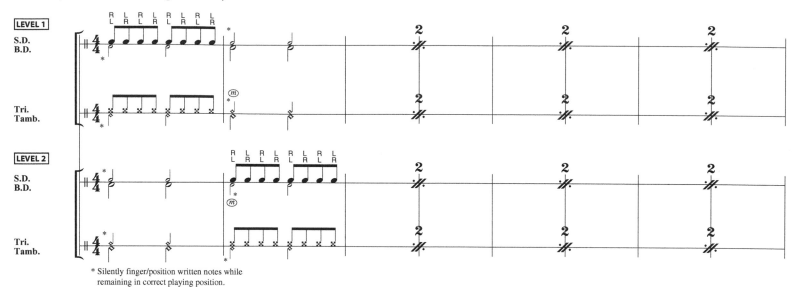

* Silently finger/position written notes while
  remaining in correct playing position.

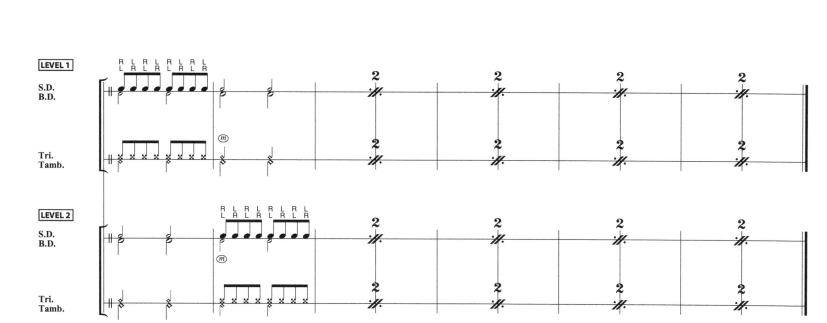

Percussion Goals

Level 1

1. Breathe together.
2. Start together.
3. Strike the instrument in the same place, with the same **energy** every time.
4. Where applicable, dampen to **match** the ends of the wind players' notes.
5. Match the articulation style/dynamic level of the wind players.
6. **Organize** the ends of notes before "shadowing" as clearly as the beginning of the next note actually played.
7. Breathe on count 3 before entrances
8. This exercise can be practiced with single strokes or rolls.
9. Listen to make sure that the **balance** to the wind players remains constant.

A 10. Auxiliary percussion should produce the same **color** of sound every time.

Level 2

P,K,T 1. Hand, wrist and arm movement should be smooth and fluid.

8. Extending Skills in Upper Register

8–1 Ascending Concert F Scale (Two-Note Segments)

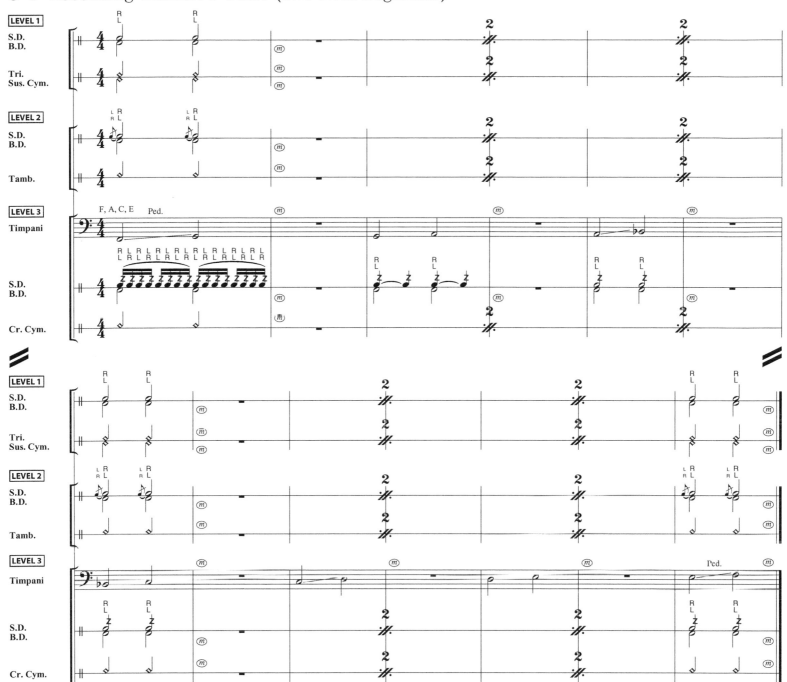

 Percussion Goals

Level 1

1. Breathe together.
2. Start together.
3. Strike the instrument in the same place, with the same **energy** every time.
4. Where applicable, dampen to **match** the ends of the wind players' notes.
5. The second note of any two-note pattern should be the same volume as the first.
6. Breathe on count 3 before entrances
7. Listen to make sure that the **balance** to the wind players remains constant.

A   8. Auxiliary percussion should produce the same **color** of sound every time.

Level 2/3

P   1. All flams should have the same quality of sound.
P   2. Rolls should have a smooth beginning and end, without extraneous noise.
K   3. Notes played in octaves should sound at exactly the same time; subdivide internally.
T   4. Pedaling should occur (fast) just before the mallet strikes the head.
K,T 5. Rolls should be smooth and even, without extraneous noise.

Boldface words are terms that can be found in the glossary at the back of the book.

Goal Key: **P**=Snare, Bass Drum and Cymbals; **K**=Keyboard; **A**=Auxiliary; **T**=Timpani

ⓜ = Muffle (dampen)

8–2 Ascending Concert F Scale – WW Model/Brass Lip Vibrations (Four and Eight-Note Segments)

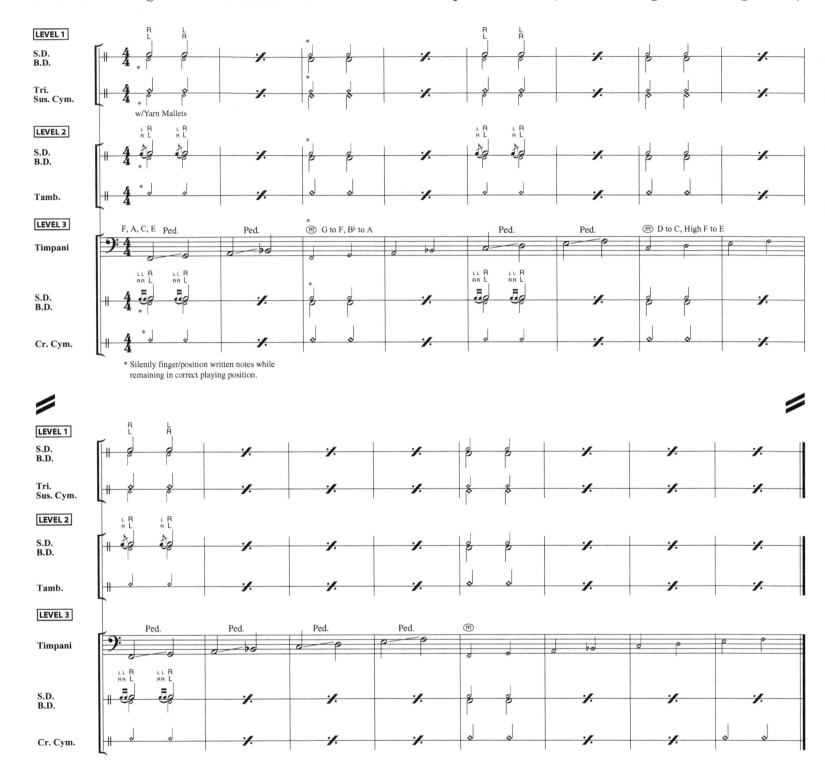

* Silently finger/position written notes while
remaining in correct playing position.

 ### Percussion Goals (for 8–2 and 8–3)

Level 1
1. Breathe together.
2. Start together.
3. Strike the instrument in the same place, with the same **energy** every time.
4. Where applicable, dampen to **match** the ends of the wind players' notes.
5. Breathe on count 3 before entrances.
6. Listen to make sure that the **balance** to the wind players remains constant.
7. This exercise can be practiced with single strokes or rolls. (**8–3** only)

A 8. Auxiliary percussion should produce the same **color** of sound every time.

Level 2/3
P 1. All flams and ruffs should have the same quality of sound throughout.
K 2. Notes played in octaves should sound at exactly the same time; subdivide internally.
T 3. Pedaling should occur (fast) just before the mallet strikes the head.
K,T 4. Rolls should be smooth and even, without extraneous noise.

8–3 Ascending Concert F Scale – WW Model (Triple Rhythms)/Brass on Instruments
(Four and Eight-Note Segments)

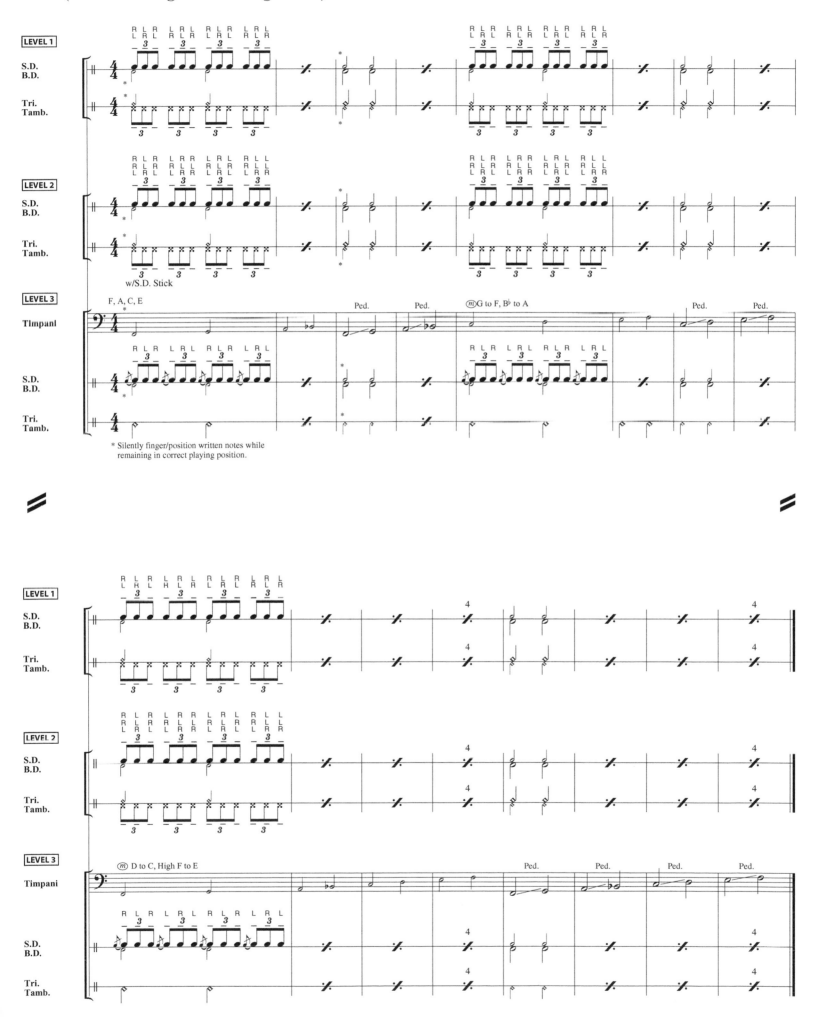

* Silently finger/position written notes while
remaining in correct playing position.

8–4 Complete Ascending Concert F Scale – WW Model/Brass Lip Vibrations (Two-Note Segments)

Percussion Goals

Level 1
1. Breathe together.
2. Start together.
3. Strike the instrument in the same place, with the same **energy** every time.
4. Where applicable, dampen to **match** the ends of the wind players' notes.
5. Match the articulation style/dynamic level of the wind players.
6. Breathe on count 3 before entrances
7. Listen to make sure that the **balance** to the wind players remains constant.
    A   8. Auxiliary percussion should produce the same **color** of sound every time.

Level 2/3
  P   1. All flams should have the same quality of sound.
  K   2. Notes played in octaves should sound at exactly the same time; subdivide internally.
  T   3. Pedaling should occur (fast) just before the mallet strikes the head.
K,T 4. Rolls should be smooth and even, without extraneous noise.

This page intentionally left blank to facilitate page turn.

8–5 Complete Ascending Concert F Scale – WW Model (Duple Rhythms)/Brass Half Notes

* Silently finger/position written notes while
  remaining in correct playing position.

Percussion Goals

Level 1

1. Breathe together.
2. Start together.
3. Strike the instrument in the same place, with the same **energy** every time.
4. Where applicable, dampen to **match** the ends of the wind players' notes.
5. Match the articulation style/dynamic level of the wind players.
6. Breathe on count 3 before entrances.
7. This exercise can be practiced with single strokes or rolls.
8. Listen to make sure that the **balance** to the wind players remains constant.
   A 9. Auxiliary percussion should produce the same **color** of sound every time.

Level 2/3

P 1. All flams should have the same quality of sound.
K 2. Notes played in octaves should sound at exactly the same time; subdivide internally.
T 3. Pedaling should occur (fast) just before the mallet strikes the head.

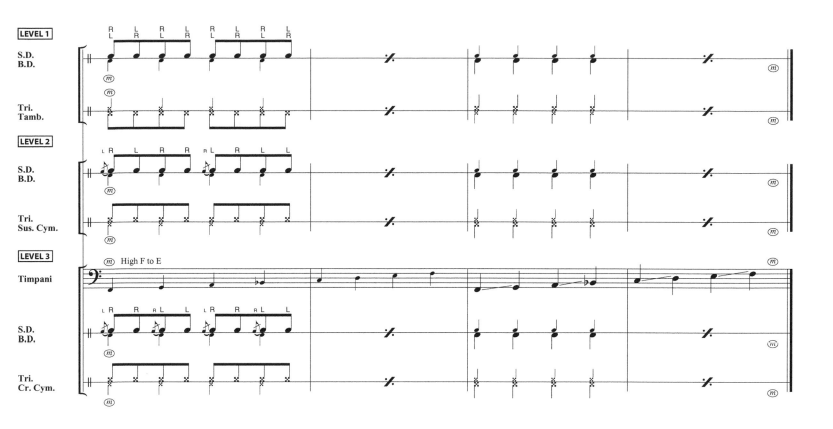

9. Combining Elements

Percussion Goals (9–1)

Level 1
1. Breathe together.
2. Start together.
3. Strike the instrument in the same place, with the same **energy** every time.
4. Where applicable, dampen to **match** the ends of the wind players' notes.
5. Breathe on count 4 quarter rests.

Level 2/3

P	1.	All flams and ruffs should have the same quality of sound throughout.
P	2.	Snare drum roll speed (16th note, 8th note, 16th note triplet base) should be determined by the tempo.
K	3.	Notes played in octaves should sound at exactly the same time; subdivide internally.
K	4.	When playing rolls in octaves, they should be tonally even, hand-to-hand.
P,K,T	5.	Rolls should be smooth and even, without extraneous noise.

Boldface words are terms that can be found in the glossary at the back of the book.

Goal Key: **P**=Snare, Bass Drum and Cymbals; **K**=Keyboard; **A**=Auxiliary; **T**=Timpani

ⓜ = Muffle (dampen)

9–1 Ascending/Descending Parallel Intervals
(Goals on p.109)

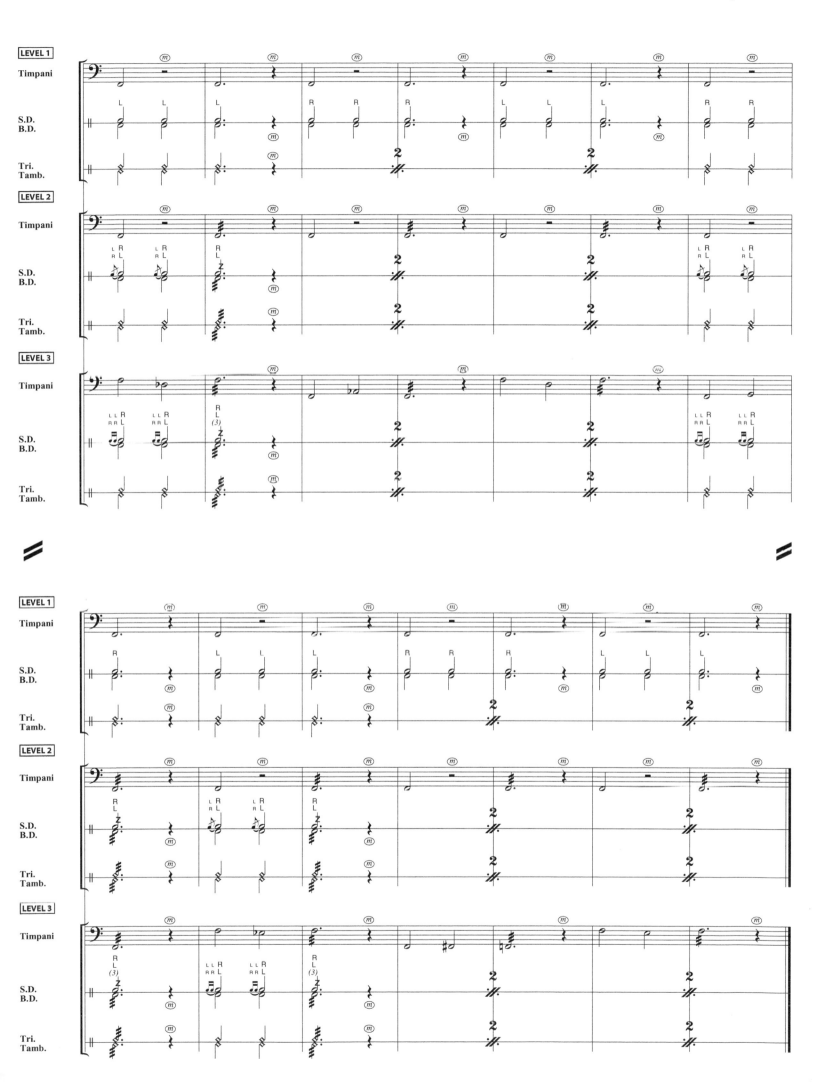

9–2 Combined Ascending/Descending Intervals

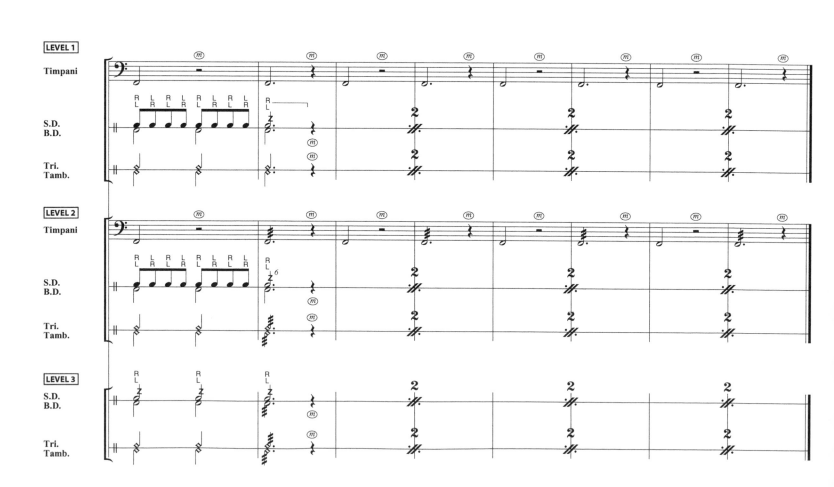

Percussion Goals

Level 1

1. Breathe together.
2. Start together.
3. Strike the instrument in the same place, with the same **energy** every time.
4. Do not accent the beginnings of rolls.
5. Rolls should be smooth and even, without extraneous noise.
6. Where applicable, dampen to **match** the ends of the wind players' notes.
7. Match the articulation style/dynamic level of the winds.
8. Hand, wrist, and arm motions should look smooth and fluid.
9. This exercise can be practiced with single strokes or rolls.
10. Breathe on count 4 quarter rests.

P   11. Snare drum roll speed (16th note, 8th note, 16th note triplet base) should be determined by the tempo.

K,T 12. As the interval expands, the notes should have the same tonal qualities.

Level 2/3

P   1. Snare drum stroke height during the roll should be consistent.

K   2. Notes played in octaves should sound at exactly the same time; subdivide internally.

K   3. When rolling two different notes at the same time, both notes should match dynamically and tonally.

9-3 Descending Parallel Fifths

Percussion Goals

Level 1

1. Breathe together.
2. Start together.
3. Strike the instrument in the same place, with the same **energy** every time.
4. Do not accent the beginnings of rolls.
5. **Match** the articulation style/dynamic level of the winds.
6. As the interval expands, the notes should have the same tonal qualities.
7. Where applicable, dampen to match the ends of the wind players' notes.
8. This exercise can be practiced with single strokes or rolls.
9. Breathe on count 4 quarter rests.

P 10. Snare drum roll speed (16th note, 8th note, 16th note triplet base) should be determined by the tempo.

Level 2/3

P 1. Snare drum stroke height during the roll should be consistent.

K 2. Notes played in octaves should sound at exactly the same time; subdivide internally.

K 3. When rolling two different notes at the same time, both notes should match dynamically and tonally.

9–4 Ascending Parallel Fifths

Percussion Goals

Level 1

1. Breathe together.
2. Start together.
3. Strike the instrument in the same place, with the same **energy** every time.
4. Do not accent the beginnings of rolls.
5. **Match** the articulation style/dynamic level of the winds.
6. Where applicable, dampen to match the ends of the wind players' notes.
7. This exercise can be practiced with single strokes or rolls.
8. Breathe on count 4 quarter rests.

P 9. Snare drum roll speed (16th note, 8th note, 16th note triplet base) should be determined by the tempo.

Level 2/3

P 1. Snare drum stroke height during the roll should be consistent.

K 2. Notes played in octaves should sound at exactly the same time; subdivide internally.

K 3. When rolling two different notes at the same time, both notes should match dynamically and tonally.

10. Learning to Play Cadences

10–1 Outlining a Chord Progression With Pedal Tone

Shake Roll or Thumb Roll

Percussion Goals
Level 1

1. Breathe together.
2. Start together.
3. Release together.
4. **Match** the line tonally, with the same **energy**/dynamic level.
5. Rolls should be smooth and even, without extraneous noise.
6. The hand, wrist and arm motion should look the same hand-to-hand.
7. Line A should be played musically, with direction and motion.
8. Line A – keep the volume consistent from note to note.
9. Line A – breathe on count 4 quarter rests.

A 10. Triangle and tambourine: each should have a consistent quality of sound, note-to-note.

Level 2/3

P 1. All ruffs should have the same quality of sound throughout.
P 2. Rolls should be smooth and even, without extraneous noise.
P 3. Crash cymbals should produce the same **color** of sound throughout.
K 4. When playing the two note rolls, the moving note should not be stronger or weaker than the **pedal tone**.

Boldface words are terms that can be found in the glossary at the back of the book.

Goal Key: **P**=Snare, Bass Drum and Cymbals; **K**=Keyboard; **A**=Auxiliary; **T**=Timpani

ⓜ = Muffle (dampen)

11. Learning Even Note-Valued Technique
11–1 thru 20 Percussion Tacet

Percussion Preface

Today's percussionist has increasingly higher technical and musical demands placed upon them at all levels of development. They perform on a wide variety of instruments, with a multitude of mallets. It is imperative that percussionists develop organizational skills to coordinate the physical and mental demands of the many instruments.

How to Approach Percussion with 'Ensemble Concepts'

Ensemble Concepts will cover varying degrees of percussion performance. Each exercise will contain one to three levels. Each level will have specific goals addressing skills needed to perform in a band or percussion ensemble. The levels offer students a range of technical challenges.

These exercises are designed to develop mental awareness of what is needed physically to produce a desired **tone color** from their instrument. Most exercises include basic percussion instruments used in band literature. Decisions concerning which instruments and levels to implement should be determined by the ensemble's concert repertoire. Percussionists should rotate through the various instruments throughout the week. It is not necessary to include all parts every day. *Ensemble Concepts* can also be used in sectionals, where various techniques can be closely monitored.

Mallet and stick selection should be decided by the director. Generally, avoid mallets that are very hard and articulate. A good quality, medium to medium-soft mallet will suffice for all keyboard instruments and timpani. A good quality concert stick should be used on the snare. Always try to provide the best quality mallets and instruments your budget will allow. It is very difficult, if not impossible, to replicate professional sounds with inferior equipment.

These exercises are not intended to cover all areas of percussion performance. Instruments such as toms, wood block, claves, conga drums, chimes, etc., can optionally be used.

All information included in the wind instrument books is applicable to percussion performance. Be aware of how percussion relates to the total ensemble. The goal, regardless of instrument or level, is to have a mental awareness of the physical skills necessary to produce the desired tone color, and their musical role in the ensemble.

Balance Essentials

Percussionists have a unique role in the ensemble. While wind players produce sounds through a combination of air and vibrations, percussionists create sounds by striking an object with a hand or mallet. Understanding this, it is vital to possess the mental awareness of what should be done physically to create the many possible tone colors.

Many factors are involved to create sounds a conductor may desire. The size of the instrument, tension of the heads and mallet/stick selection are some of the decisions that should be made. There is an endless array of percussion sounds that can be created. Understand what tone color is appropriate, and work towards that end.

Generally, percussion sections tend to be too loud. This happens because they do not understand their role in the ensemble. When **balancing** any ensemble, the percussionists should know how their parts relate within their section, as well as the rest of the ensemble.

Percussionists should think of **balance** as "layers" of **color**, not colors blended together. Rarely are percussion parts doubled. Therefore, every percussionist is a soloist to some degree. Percussion parts are written either to enhance a wind player's part, to create a **timbre** that is unique or for effect.

No other section can match percussion's unique variety of timbres. The conductor should consider the projection capabilities for each instrument. For example, a triangle can be heard very easily, regardless of volume, due to its distinct sound. Toms, on the other hand, tend to get lost in the ensemble sound due to the heads having too little tension, or played with a soft mallet that is not articulate enough.

By having the percussion **fitting into** a particular wind sound, it raises their mental awareness of their role in the ensemble. Balancing entails **matching tonal energy**, articulation, releases and moving together rhythmically. It applies to the percussion section as significantly as it does to any other section.

Organizing the Percussion Section

Organizing the Equipment
- Have places for all of the equipment
- Storage cabinets are necessary – they can be purchased or home made
- Have covers for all equipment (store bought or home made)
- Have cases for all equipment for protection during transportation.
- Assign students responsibilities for equipment
- Label all equipment
- The school should provided mallets for larger instruments (i.e., bass drum, gong, chimes, etc.)
- Use towels, thick fabric, or carpet over music stands used to hold mallets, accessories, etc.

General Maintenance
- Visually inspect all equipment periodically
- Students can help monitor equipment
- Have "equipment check days"
- Have replacement parts – from either a music store or a hardware store (less expensive)
- Have a basic tool kit
- Stock small items (washers, screws, nuts, bolts, felts, cymbal sleeves, lubricants, etc.)
- Instruct students on how to repair equipment/replace parts

Assignments
- Use an assignment sheets/chart for all music – good time saving device
- Rotate instrument assignments – everyone plays everything
- Post a list to be rehearsed, allowing for percussion set up/planning
- Cover all instruments and put away all equipment after each rehearsal

Location
- In a band setting – place generally behind the ensemble, towards the center, extending to the left or right
- Keyboards on the outside (marimba, vibes towards the outer edges)
- Smaller drums towards the back, bass drum and timpani towards the center, near tubas and low brass
- Don't put the timpani too close to the bass drum
- Set ups will change depending on the music, the number of players and the equipment needed

Basic Percussion Techniques

Basic Concepts

- Correctness before speed – speed is a by-product of correct technique
- Develop technique by "slow-fast-slow" or "open-closed-open" methods
- Staying relaxed is a priority – neck, shoulders, arms, wrists and hands
- Sticks should be balanced hand-to-hand, both visually and audibly
- Fingers always remain in contact with the stick
- Sticks strike the drum close to each other – within 1 bead width
- Practice different ways (hands-apart, RH only, LH only, etc.)
- The slower the technique, the higher the sticks
- The faster the technique, the lower the sticks
- Practice at all levels of dynamics and speed
- Softer dynamics require lower stick heights (1" – 3")
- Louder dynamics require higher stick heights (4" – 9")
- Create the same tone stroke-to-stroke and hand-to-hand

Single Strokes

- Single non alternating: RRRRRRRRR or LLLLLLLLL
- Single alternating RLRLRLRLRL or LRLRLRLRL

Double Strokes

- RH start – RRLLRRLLRRLL
- LH start – LLRRLLRRLLRR

Rolls

- How a drum sustains a sound

Concert Rolls (Multiple Bounce Rolls, Buzz Rolls)

- Use just enough pressure on the stick to create a fulcrum
- Allow the stick to bounce freely on the drum
- The last three fingers start slightly away from stick, but stay curled and relaxed
- As the bounces close up (get faster), apply slight pressure to grip
- Apply a light "squeeze" from the index finger to control amount of rebound
- Gradually alternate hands until the beginning and ending of the strokes overlap
- Experiment to find out what works for each student
- Do not allow the fingers to be straight beneath the hands – this creates tension
- Gradually increase the speed until a desired smooth roll is heard
- Start with short rolls, then progress to longer rolls
- Most students will have success with this fairly quickly – it is a good motivational tool

Open Roll – Rudimental Roll

- Start slowly – R R L L R R L L
- Create even sounds/strokes
- Gradually increase speed
- Stay relaxed
- Double strokes will eventually turn into rebounds
- Rebound: when there are two hits with one stroke
- Open rolls are more difficult to execute; they require significant control
- Introduce after the multiple bounce roll is established
- Start with short rolls

Roll Interpretation

- Most band music uses concert or multiple bounce rolls
- Rudimental rolls are often used in solos, marches
- Notation is not standardized between rudimental and concert rolls
- Tempo determines the base (these are approximate)
  a. slow tempo – use 16th note triplet base (60 – 90 beats per minute)
  b. medium tempo – use 16th note base (90 – 130 b.p.m.)
  c. fast tempo – use 1/8 note triplet base (130 – 180 b.p.m)
  d. very fast tempo – use 1/8 note base (180 b.p.m. and faster)
- Decisions concerning roll length are usually determined by the context of the music

Accent Studies and Concepts

- For accented notes use high strokes
- For unaccented notes use low strokes
- Strive to maintain a consistent sound between accented and unaccented notes
- Work accented exercises with RH and LH lead
- Keep arm motion to a minimum
- Work to control the rebound when an accent stroke is immediately followed by an unaccented stroke
- Do not "slam" accented notes

Flams

- Difficult to execute – uses two different strokes at the same time
- Two sounds – unaccented note (grace note) and accented notes (main stroke)
  a. For the grace note use a low stroke
  b. For the main note use a high stroke
  c. Both sticks start and stop at the same time (Important)
- Both strokes are controlled (the hands and wrists should remain relaxed)
- The lower stroke will hit first and sound softer; the main stroke follows almost immediately, and is louder
- Both sticks strike almost at the same time
- It sounds just like it is said: "flam" not "fa-lam"
- Work the same lead hand flams: lR, lR, lR; then: rL, rL, rL; for consistent timing and sound
- Gradually add alternations with rest in between:
  a. Slow (correctness) before fast (speed)

Ruffs and Drags

- Difficult to execute – uses two different "types" of strokes at the same time
- Same basic concept as the flam – two sounds – grace notes (rr or ll) and the main stroke
- The grace notes are bounced (1 wrist action = 2 bounces), the main stroke is controlled
- "Open sound" – the double bounced grace note can be heard clearly
- "Closed sound" – the double bounced grace notes have a sustained sound
- Sticks start and stop together (Important)
- The low stroke will hit first and sound softer; the main stroke follows almost immediately and is louder.
- Both sticks strike almost at the same time

Four Stroke Ruff

- Sounds like a double stroke ruff: llR or rrL
- Played with alternating grace notes: lrlR or rlrL (most common stickings)
- Can be played with different stickings: lrlR, rlrL, rllR,lrrL, rrlR, llrL
- Uses the same concept as flams in regard to sound, single development, etc.

Special Effects

- Composers sometimes call for special "sound" effects
  a. Rim shot (Hit the rim and head at the same time)
  b. Stick on stick rim shot (Place one stick down on the head, bead in the center of the head, and the butt over the counter hoop; then strike with the remaining stick)
  c. Knock (Place the bead of the stick on the head and strike the shaft on the rim)
  d. Play on rim
  e. Play on shell
  f. Use of brushes
  g. Experiment with different areas for different sounds

Timpani – Basic Information

Construction

- Normal head diameters are 32", 29", 26", 23" and 20"
- Copper bowls (either smooth or hand hammered) create the best tonal qualities
- Fiberglass bowls are cheaper, but do not sound as good as copper bowls
- The bowl acts as a resonator for the vibrating head and enclosed air chamber
- Suspended bowls with extended collars offer the best **resonance**
- Pedal tuned timpani are preferable for fast tuning changes
- Exterior tuning mechanisms are preferable for the best tone
- Tuning gauges should be purchased if at all possible
- Heads:
  a. A good quality plastic head is acceptable for general school use
  b. "Synthetic" calf skin head offers the best tonal resonance
  c. Calf skin heads are not a good choice (high maintenance)
  d. Replace the heads every year, budget permitting

Mallets

- Have a variety of good quality mallets available (soft, medium, hard, very hard)
- Have a variety of different shafts available – wood, bamboo, metal
- Timpani head felts are available in seamless and seamed models
- Mark seamed mallets with a dot on the seam – avoid playing on the seam
- Keep mallets in a plastic bag or mallet bag for protection
- Avoid touching the felts – hand oils attract dirt, which promotes "pilling"

Positioning

- 2 drums – Have the pedals almost parallel to each other, and facing the player
- Face the intersection of the two drums; this is where music stand is placed
- When adding drums, be careful not to position them too closely to the player; the drums should form a wide arc
- Sit or stand – determined by the height of the player
- A stool is necessary for a lot of pedal work
- If a stool is used, the feet should rest on the floor, or lightly on the pedals

Playing Areas

- The basic playing area is 4" – 5" inside the edge of the bowl
- Playing spots are determined by the quality of sound; some adjustment may be necessary
- Musical demands may require a change of playing area

Tuning the Desired Pitches

- Use a three step method:
    a. Play the **pitch** (keyboard, pitch pipe, tuning fork)
    b. Sing the pitch
    c. Starting at the lowest note, keep the ear close to the drum head to hear the fundamental; gently stroke the head and quickly glissando up to match the pitch

Tuning Exercises

- Use a sequenced method
- A good source is from method books
- Establish the 4ths and 5ths first, then proceed inwardly and outwardly
- Use the opening interval of familiar melodies to help recognize intervals

Performance Tuning

- It is difficult to tune and not get lost in the music
- It helps if the player can sing all of the required intervals – in sequence of the music
- Determine the pitch from the last pitch sounding – the player should recognize intervals
- Play the pitches and check the tuning in the rhythm of the music
- Listen to the ensemble for the needed notes – particularly the tubas
- Recognize "out of tune" notes and make quick adjustments while playing
- Do not hit so loudly as to be heard above the ensemble

Tuning Gauges

- Gauges are very helpful
- Gauges should be checked and adjusted before a rehearsal or performance
- Use the gauges as an aid to get close; they should not be totally relied on
- There are many types available – pedal attached, cable attached, electronic, homemade

Timpani Techniques

Grips

- There are two basic grips:
    a. German grip – a variation is called the "American" grip
        1. Equated with a "dark" quality of sound
        2. Palms are turned slightly inward, towards one another
    b. French Grip – sometimes called the "thumbs up" grip
        1. Equated with a "light" quality of sound
        2. Palms will be facing in, towards one other
        3. Thumbs should be on top of the mallet
- All grips are held toward the back ends of the mallet with about 1" extending beyond the hand (Important concept)
- The tip of the index finger should be curled slightly around the shaft
- The side of the thumb should be positioned relatively close to the base of the index finger
- The thumb and index finger should be opposite of each other on the shaft
- Regardless of the grip, the hands should look natural and relaxed

Stroke Development

- Proper stroke development comes from "watching–listening–doing" and mental awareness of what happens physically to achieve the desired tone
- Use of the "total" body is more important with timpani than with other percussion
- Relax the neck, shoulders, arms and wrists
- The fingers should stay in contact with shaft
- "Air drumming" is a good developmental exercise

Basic Stroke

- Piston stroke – full stroke
- The mallet should come back off the drum; do not hinder this motion
- Get used to the natural rebound, this is most important in stroke development
- Do not grip the mallet too tightly
- Strive for a full **resonant** tone
- Use the "bouncing ball" analogy
- Use the hand, wrist and arm in a smooth, natural motion
- Practice legato strokes first
- Work the hands separately
- Make the same sounds with different hands – **match** them tonally
- Use the "arc" concept of motion, drum to drum
- The use of mirrors and/or video tape is very helpful
- Larger timpani requires a slightly stronger stroke

Roll Concepts

- Single stroke rolls are used to sustain note values
- The range of the drum determines speed of roll:
  - a. Higher notes require faster rolls, lower notes require slower rolls
  - b. Higher drums require faster rolls, lower drums require slower rolls
- A metered rhythmic pulse (individual notes) should not be heard
- Rolls should have a smooth start, good follow through and a smooth ending, unless they start and/or end with an accent

Muffling

- Place the pinky, ring and middle fingers on the head to stop it from vibrating
- Use entering long, extended rests, and the end of a piece
- Use when convenient to stop a note from "leaking" into the next note
- Different techniques:
  - a. Muffle the last tone with the hand that played it
  - b. Muffle the last tone with the opposite hand
  - c. Muffle both drums with a hand on each drum
  - d. Muffle, combining the above techniques
- Muffling should not cause extraneous noises

Muting

- Place a small piece of felt, cloth or suede on the head
- Suede material works well
- Different degrees of muting:
  - a. Placed in the center – muting will be minimum
  - b. Placed towards the edge – muting will be moderate
  - c. Placed halfway between the center and the edge – maximum muting
- Experiment to achieve the tone desired

Articulation Considerations

- Use legato strokes for fullness of tone
- Use staccato strokes for fast articulated passages
- Considerations:
    a. The height of the stroke – changes in volume
    b. How the stroke is made – changes in style
    c. Where to play on the head – relationship of drums and vibration of playing area
    d. Knowing what sound is expected

Sticking policies

- There are four sticking policies:
    a. Crossing (least desirable – avoid when possible)
    b. Shifting or swing sticking
    c. Doubling – depends on direction of movement
    d. Alternating
- Sticking guidelines
    a. Even number of strokes moving to the left – begin with left
    b. Even number of strokes moving to the right – begin with right
    c. Odd number of strokes moving to the left – begin with right
    d. Odd number of strokes moving to the right – begin with left
- Mark the music with R for right, L for Left, X for cross-stick and for swing sticking

Snare Drum – Basic Information

The **tonal color** of a snare drum will vary according to size, depth, construction, head selection (top and bottom), head tensioning and type of stick used. Here are some examples to consider:

Size

- Concert snare drum – 14" diameter with various depth of shells
- Parade or marching snare – 14" or 15" diameter x 12" deep shell
- Piccolo snare drum – 14" or 13" diameter x 3" deep shell (approximate depth)

Construction

- Wood shell
- Metal – assorted (i.e., bronze, chrome plated, hand hammered, etc.)
- Fiberglass

Heads

- Natural skin – not practical for school use
- Mylar/plastic – preferred
- Batter head (top)
- Snare head (bottom)

Snares

- For a variety of tonal colors use the following snares:
    a. Gut
    b. Wire (most common)
    c. Nylon
    d. Cable
    e. Combinations of above (available on some models)

Sticks

- Sticks are made from different materials; wood is preferable
- There are many different brands and models to choose from:
  a. Weight and size of stick determine the tone color
  b. Use the appropriate size for the type of sound desired
     1. Use medium weight/diameter sticks for most school uses
     2. Light, small diameter sticks for small, thin sounds
     3. Heavier, thicker sticks for full-bodied sounds
- Selection
  a. Roll the sticks on flat surface to check for warping
  b. Check that sticks match pitch
  c. Check that the grain is smooth and free of flaws

Playing Areas

- Center – dry, slightly muffled tone
- Off center – full tone with the most **resonance**
- Edge – thin, unfocused
- Tonal considerations dictate the playing area, not dynamics (Important concept)
- Always play over the snares for optimum clarity

Instrument Height

- Should be level (matched grip) or tilted slightly (traditional grip)
- Batter (top) should be just below belt level – this is approximate
- In playing position, arms should angle down slightly, away from the body

Stance

- Weight should be equally distributed to both feet
- The body should be in a relaxed, comfortable position
- The shoulders should be down, rounded and relaxed
- Avoid any type of body tension or stiffness
- The elbows should be slightly behind the spinal column
- Don't stand too close to the instrument

Tuning

- Snare head should be pitched slightly higher that the batter head
- Snare tension should have a crisp sound heard at all dynamic levels

Grips

Matched Grip

- Advantages
  a. Both hands – same grip
  b. Both hands do the same thing (stroke)
  c. The same muscles control each hand
  d. Grip applies to other percussion instruments
- Disadvantages
  a. Most students are right handed, so the left hand is weaker

Matched Grip Hand Position

- Grip the stick about 1/3 away from the butt with the thumb and index finger
- The thumb should rest along the shaft of the stick across from the index finger
- The stick should rest between the first joint of the index finger and thumb
- The index finger should point down
- The stick should cross the hand at fleshy part of palm
- The remaining fingers should curve naturally and gently touch the stick
- The palms should be parallel to floor
- The hands should be slightly in front of the body, about waist level
- The beads of the sticks should be about 1/2" apart
- The sticks should form a "V"

Traditional Grip

- Advantages
    a. The left hand is generally weaker – more muscles are used in the left hand
- Disadvantages
    a. This grip does not transfer to other percussion instruments
    b. There are different stroke concepts from hand to hand

Traditional Grip Hand Position

- Hold palm of the left hand facing towards you
- Curl the fingers in (about halfway)
- Lay the stick across the hand, butt end sticking out approximately 1" from the thumb base (fleshy part)
- Rest the stick shaft between the 1st and 2nd joint of the ring finger
- The middle finger should be relaxed and extended over top of the stick
- The index finger curls over the stick on top
- The first joint of the thumb touches the first joint of the index finger
- The hand should be positioned slightly in front of the body, a little below the waist
- The palm of the hand should be perpendicular to the floor, and facing the right hand
- The right hand should be the same as the matched grip

Snare Drum Sticking Policies and Patterns

Sticking Policies

- Advantages to having a sticking policy
    a. Gives students a reference base
    b. Aids in reading music patterns
    c. Improves the sound evenness
    d. Helps increase uniformity and precision
    e. Achieves greater rhythmic stability
- Students should be familiar with all sticking policies and their appropriate use with each instrument
- Students should mark stickings on their music – this will help them stroke the same way every time

Four Basic Sticking Policies

- Right Hand Lead – base is RLRL for 16th note patterns
- Left Hand Lead – base is LRLR for 16th note patterns
- Alternation – based upon alternation RLRLRL, regardless of the rhythmic structure
- Doubling – use of double strokes to help facilitate movement and shifting

Rudiments

- Develop all rudiments for control and technical development
- Be familiar with the Percussive Arts Society's "40 Rudiments"
- Use all stickings as marked
- Use stickings reflecting the composer's intent

Having a sticking policy is very important during the early stages of percussion study. It establishes a foundation that transfers to all percussion instruments. Also, rudiment study cannot be stressed enough. Diligent rudiment practice will help all areas of development.

Keyboard Percussion – Basic Information

Xylophone

- Bars made from rosewood or synthetic material
- Mallet selections include hard rubber, plastic, polyball, wood, acrylic
    a. On wood bars – use rubber, soft plastic or wood mallets
    b. Never use brass mallets on a xylophone
    c. Birch or rattan handles – personal preference
- Use good brand name mallet
- Sound characteristics:
    a. Crisp, articulate
    b. Fast decay
    c. Fast rolls, needed to sustain sound
    d. Very rhythmic
    e. Played over resonators, slightly off center, or on the edges of the bars (sharps/flats)
    f. Avoid playing on the nodes (where the string goes through the bars)

Marimba

- Variety of yarn mallets (soft – hard)
- Some rubber mallets (not hard)
- Low range – soft mallets (depending on projection)
- Medium range – medium mallets (depending on projection)
- Upper range – hard mallets (depending on projection)
- Mallets can have birch or rattan handles (personal preference)
- Use good brand name mallets for the marimba
- Sound characteristics:
    a. Dark and mellow
    b. **Resonant** low and medium registers
    c. Articulate with a fast decay in the upper register
- Difficult to hear in a full band setting (often play a dynamic level louder)
- Use of four mallets (multiple mallets) is increasingly popular at all levels
- Capable of many "moods"
- Play over resonators, slightly off center, or on the edges of the bars (sharps/flats)
- Avoid playing on the nodes (where the string goes through the bars)

Vibraphone (Vibraharp or Vibes)

- Variety of cord or yarn mallets (soft – medium – hard)
- Some rubber mallets (soft – medium – hard)
- Mallets can have birch or rattan handles (usually cord wound)
- Use good quality mallets for vibes

- Use of four mallets (multiple mallets) is increasingly popular at all levels
- Capable of many sound effects (i.e., use of rotors, glissandos, pitch bending, use of bow, etc.)
- Play over resonators, slightly off center, or on the edges of the bars (sharps/flats)
- Avoid playing on the nodes (where string goes through bars)
- Sound characteristics:
    a. Wide spectrum of sounds, from dark and mellow to bright and shimmery
    b. Strong third overtone (double octave)
- Sustained sound and dampening through use of a foot pedal
- Mallet dampening techniques are also used
- Difficult to hear in a full band setting (often play a dynamic level louder)
- Composers sometimes specify "motor on/off"
- Play over resonators, slightly off center, or on the edges of the bars (sharps/flats)
- Avoid playing on the nodes (where the string goes through the bars)

Glockenspiel or Concert Bells

- Hard rubber, plastic, polyball, acrylic, brass (use sparingly/carefully)
- Mallets can have birch or rattan handles (avoid fiberglass shafts)
- Have a good assortment of mallets available for bells (multiple pairs – from soft to hard)
- Use good quality mallets for bells
- Sound characteristics:
    a. Bright, brilliant sound
    b. Can easily be heard
- Mallet technique requires a quick rebound from the bar to achieve maximum tone
- Hand dampening is often used
- Generally, do not roll unless instructed to do so
- Playing area – generally in the center or edges of the bars

Keyboard Percussion Techniques

Concepts

- The grip is very similar to the matched grip
- The stroke is similar to the basic percussion stroke
- Some minor adjustments to the stroke are necessary
- Establish an correct "area" for each concept
- Introduce one concept at a time
- Student should be aware of "how it feels" to execute each concept (mental awareness)
- "Awareness" instructions are better than "do this" instructions

Grip

- Basically the same as the matched grip
- Hold near the end of the shaft with no more than 1" extending beyond the base of the hand
- Grip the shaft between the thumb and the first joint of the index finger (the shaft is smaller than a snare drum stick)
- Do not allow the shaft to slip to a resting point between the middle joint of the index finger and the thumb
- The remaining three fingers remain relaxed around the shaft, but do not let more than 1" of space occur between the fingers and the palm of hand while playing

Stroke Concepts

- The wrist controls the stroke, with little arm or finger motion
- The back of the hands are up, with palms parallel to the floor

- Body position is the same as for snare – feel balanced and centered
- Elbows are relaxed at the side of the body
- Pinky fingers almost touching the bars indicate a correct hand height
- The left mallet is in front of the right mallet, above the center of the bar (this is a general concept and will depend on sticking-related issues)
- Avoid stooping, bending over or tiptoeing to accommodate correct playing height
    a. Raise the instrument by placing blocks under wheels
    b. Raise the student by building a platform
- The body should be positioned within the middle range of the instrument
- Body weight should be distributed evenly over both feet
- Shoulders are parallel to the instrument – try not to reach
- Shuffle the feet to move to different playing positions – do not move by crossing the feet over

Playing Areas of Bars

- The center of the bar produces the maximum fundamental tone and less harmonic presence
- Play slightly off center or near the end of the bar to produce more harmonic presence and less fundamental tone
- Do not play on the "node" unless specified by the composer
- Musical and technical considerations come into play when selecting playing areas
- Good rule of thumb:
    a. On the natural notes – strike off center (towards the accidental notes)
    b. On the accidental notes – strike on the extreme ends closest to the natural notes
- Use different areas to facilitate ease of technique
- Keep **tone color** and musical expression as main considerations

Concepts of Expression and Phrasing

In order to achieve optimum levels of expression and phrasing, proficiency of the full stroke technique and understanding the concepts of tone production and sticking policies are necessary.

Advanced Keyboard Percussion Concepts

- How tones are affected by angle, style and velocity of strokes
- Striking area on the bars
- Mental/aural picture of the music
- Harmonic structure
- Phrase direction
- Attitude towards expression
- Distinguishing between legato and staccato strokes
- Dynamic and rhythmic directions of line
- Listen and study performances by keyboard percussion artists
- Avoiding muscular tension when projecting a certain style

Keyboard Percussion – Stroke and Roll Concepts

Basic Approach

- Before formal training begins, the student should become familiar with the entire keyboard
- Use scales, melodies, etc., in all ranges
- Follow with "full stroke exercises" in all ranges
- Use memorization, sequential patterns, melodies by ear and rote exercises
- Instruction and practice follows for the development of technique, reading and musical proficiency
- Stick positions/concepts of movement (this is a generalized concept and can change due to sticking issues and the ascending or descending direction of the music)

Basic Stroke

- Similar to the basic stroke with minor adjustments
- Lack of natural rebound is the major difference between keyboard and battery percussion
- Keyboard technique is based on a wrist stroke with minor arm and finger motions
- Use the lowest register for maximum tonal feedback
- Use of correct stance/body and hand position is important
- Development and toning of the wrists is important to "muscle memory"
- Development of the rebound aspects of the stroke is vital
- Students should understand the "method of movement" concepts

Full Stroke Technique

- Also referred to as a "piston stroke"
- Lift the mallets to a full stroke position, 6"-8" above the bars, bending only the wrist; strike the bar and return to the starting position in one smooth motion
- The grip remains supportive, but relaxed
- Keep the neck, shoulders, wrists and forearms relaxed
- Wrist motion resembles "bouncing a ball" or waving
- Use a full stroke in all beginning exercises
- Work for a consistent sound, look and feel
- "Correctness" before speed – speed comes from "correctness"
- Play at different dynamics (starting at different heights) and speed
- Lateral movement is done by the arms with wrist strokes
- Mental awareness of "how it feels" to produce desired tone is important

Touch-Lift Stroke

- Develops sensitivity to touch and rebound
- If the student demonstrates good touch and control, do not practice the touch-lift exercises
- This is an exercise to develop proper technique (good for glockenspiel playing)
- Begin with mallet head 1" – 2" above bar; "touch" the mallet to the bar, and with a quick and relaxed rebound, "lift" away
- Use the wrist only
- The volume will be soft due to low height
- The stroke ends with wrist bent upward and the mallet head pointing diagonally upward

Watch Out For:

- No forearm movement
- Mallet remains relaxed and almost parallel to the bars
    a. The last three fingers should not move away from the palm
    b. The shaft should not slip up to the middle joint of the index finger

- When starting, the palms face the floor
- When stopping, the back of the hands are up
- After completing the stroke, the mallet is repositioned low over the bar for the next stroke

Rolls

- Unmetered, single stroke rolls are used on keyboard instruments to sustain notes
- Vibraphone, bells and chimes can be an exception due to long vibration times
- Development of single stroke rolls is through controlled practice of single strokes, starting slowly and gradually speeding up,while remaining relaxed, then gradually slowing down
- Use short rolls before proceeding to longer rolls
- Roll speed is determined by several factors:
    a. In the upper register, the roll speed is fast
    b. In the lower register, the roll speed is slower
    c. Roll speed is faster in louder dynamics and slower in softer dynamics
    d. Musical considerations: cresendi, decrescendi
    e. **Resonance** of the instrument
    f. Movement from bar to bar
- There should be no individual (metered) strokes heard during rolls, with the exception of beginner students.

Keyboard Percussion – Multiple Mallets

Introduction of multiple mallets should begin after proficient two mallet technique is achieved. Students should learn proper grip techniques, strokes and rolls of all possible mallet combinations.

Traditional Cross Grip

Form:

- Adding a second mallet to the hand (palm facing up) between the index and middle finger
- Grasp the end of the added mallet with the pinky and ring fingers to form an anchor point on the crossed shafts
- A pivot point between the thumb and index finger is maintained whenever possible
- Spread the mallets by inserting the thumb next to the index finger inside the shaft of the first mallet and spreading the thumb and index finger apart
- To close the mallets, the pinky, ring and middle fingers squeeze the shafts together as the thumb moves back to the outside of the first mallet shaft, aiding the close
- Generally, single line notes are played with the inside mallets
- Broken lines can be distributed among all four mallets
- Generally rolls are played by a quick alternation of hands
- Advantages:
    a. Good grip for blocked cords
    b. Probably the quickest and easiest to learn
    c. Can create sound easier, with less strain
- Disadvantages:
    a. Mallet independence is minimal
    b. Large intervals are hard
    c. Large interval changes are hard
    d. Extraneous stick noises
- This technique can be used on vibes, xylophone and bells

Musser–Stevens Grip

Form:

- Second mallet inserted in the hand (palm facing up) between the middle and ring fingers and along side of the palm of the hand
- Pinky and ring fingers grasp the shaft firmly and close, curling securely into the palm
- Shafts are parallel all the way to the mallet heads
- Playing position finds the thumbnail pointing to the ceiling and mallet heads parallel to the bars
- Mallets are spread by pointing the index finger to the side and rolling the mallet shaft in away from the second mallet
- Maintain secure anchor point at all times (there should be minimal movement)
- The middle finger should keep the mallet planted in the palm of the hand
- Mallets are closed by bringing the index finger (by rolling) back to a closed position
- Generally, single note lines are played by inside mallets
- Broken lines can be played by using all four mallets
- Rolls are played by the rotation of the wrist where the mallets strike the bars in a cascading four stroke sequence
- Strokes are made by a rotary motion of the wrist, with little arm motion
- Mallets are numbered either: 1-2-3-4 (left to right or right to left)
- Advantages:
    a. Large intervals are possible
    b. Large interval changes are easier
    c. Mallet independence is good
    d. There is no extraneous noise from the mallets (shafts do not cross)
    e. Standard for many artists
- Disadvantages:
    a. Requires the ability to handle different manipulations (order) of strokes
    b. Requires the ability to manipulate two mallets independently in the same hand
- Used on marimba and vibes

The Burton Grip

Form:

- Place a mallet between the index and middle fingers
- Grip the shaft into the palm by forming a square with the middle finger and the shaft
- The middle finger anchor controls the mallets
- The other mallet is inserted through the square formed by the middle finger and the mallet shaft
- The thumb and index finger pivot point is set on the added mallet shaft
- The ring and middle fingers close lightly over the end of this shaft
- Mallets are spread by the insertion of the thumb next to the index finger inside the shaft and spreading the thumb and index finger apart – maintain the anchor on outside mallet shaft
- Mallets are closed by bringing the ring and pinky fingers toward the palm around the mallet shaft, and moving thumb back to the outside of the shaft,pushing it toward the index finger
- The ring finger will help anchor the shaft on close intervals
- Single note lines are played with inside mallets
- Broken lines are executed by all four mallets
- Roll with single hand alternations of vertical double strokes
- Advantages:
    a. Very powerful sound from all four mallets

- Disadvantages:
    a. Larger intervals are harder
    b. Large, quick interval changes are difficult
    c. Mallet independence is minimal
    d. Extraneous stick noises
- Used on vibes and marimba

Multiple Mallet Keyboard Technique

- Used to play chords and contrapuntal lines
- Concept includes rotary wrist motion with the "bouncing ball"
- Sequence of strokes:
    a. Double vertical (double vertical roll)
    b. Single independent
    c. Single alternating
    d. Double lateral (Stevens roll)
    e. Triple lateral
    f. One-handed rolls
- Correctness before speed at all levels of development

Vibraphone Technique

- With all bars the same height, double and triple sticking is used more often
- Development of pedal and mallet dampening techniques are necessary for optimum performance

Cymbals – Basic Information

Construction and Sizes (Crash and Suspended)

- Usually made from a copper/tin/bronze alloy
- 3 basic styles/weights
    a. French – light weight, fast response, light-toned, 16" – 17"
    b. Viennese – medium weight, general purpose, medium-toned, 17" – 18" (good for school use)
    c. Germanic – heavy weight , dark, low cymbals, 18" – 20"
- When spun – higher in pitch, brighter sound
- Hand hammered – lower in pitch, darker sound

Straps and Pads

- Use leather straps (best choice) – use cymbal knot to tie securely
- Do not use wood holders (screws with handles)
- Do not use pads (personal preference)
- Retie straps periodically – they will stretch
- Replace straps as needed

Grip

- Grasp the leather strap between the thumb and index finger with the side index finger firmly between the strap and cymbal

Playing Concepts

- Practice is necessary
- The desired sound is the end result of proper technique
- Use flam technique – avoid crushing or slamming together
- Work hands alone

Playing the Cymbals

- With the cymbals in hands, start with both at at 45 degree angle, comfortably in front of the body (slightly above the waist), about 1 inch apart
- One hand on top
- Strike cymbals, using the flam technique, either bottom edge/top edge or front edge/back edge
- Strike slightly off center for best results
- After striking, keep the cymbals 4-6″ apart to create resonating chamber,
- Hold the cymbals parallel to the floor with palms down; or hold the cymbals up with back of hands towards body
- Three basic motions:
    a. Prep
    b. Strike
    c. Follow through (pulled apart)
- The faster you go, the less motion you will have – mainly wrist motion
- "Shaking water off your hands" is a good motion reference
- To play softer: same technique, but with a smaller motion; start the cymbals closer together
- Prime the cymbals before playing
- A stiff body will project a stiff sound; a relaxed body will project a relaxed sound
- Muffling – after crash bring the cymbals into the body to stop ringing (vibrations)
- Use a table or cymbal caddy to rest the cymbals

Suspended Cymbal Stands

- Uses a stand: drum set stand (traditional), goose neck or boom stand
- The stand should have a metal and felt washer, cymbal sleeve, rubber feet and wing nut that fastens securely; extraneous noise will occur without these items
- Rubber tubing can be used for a cymbal sleeve
- Do not over tighten the screws
- Stay with brand name models

Suspended Cymbal Mallets

- Generally played with yarn mallets; the desired tone and response will determine what mallet is used
- Sticks, brushes, metal scrapes, triangle beaters, knitting needles, rakes, etc., are used for effects

Suspended Cymbal Playing Concepts

- Use cord or yarn keyboard mallets – composer sometimes specifies
- Playing area will be 1″ – 2″ from the edge of the cymbal
- Play opposite sides for single strokes or rolls, at the 3 and 9 o' clock positions
- Use a single stroke roll
- Roll speed will be determined by the response of cymbal and the desired tone

Bass Drum – Basic Information

Construction and Size

- A wood shell is preferable for optimum tonal characteristics
- 36″ – 40″ diameter with an minimum 18″ shell gives good depth of sound

Bass Drum Head Tuning

- Tune as low as possible (personal preference)
- The head should not sound flabby
- Tune the non-playing head slightly higher, or tune both the same (personal preference)

Bass Drum Heads

- Use a combination fiberskyn for the batter head
- Good quality plastic heads are acceptable
- Calf skin heads need a lot of care and maintenance – not for school use

Playing Areas

- Dead center – produces the lowest fundamental tone, no **resonance**
- Off center – produces a very low tone, but with more resonance and ring
- Near the edge – produces very little fundamental tone with excessive resonance
- Experiment with playing area to determine which **tone color** is desirable

Bass Drum Mallets

- Have an assortment of mallets to produce different tone colors
    a. 1 pair of general purpose mallets
    b. 1 pair of rolling mallets (generally smaller)
    c. 1 pair of hard felt mallets
    d. 1 pair of larger soft felt mallets
- Budget permitting, purchase the best quality mallets available

Playing Position

- Stand behind, not next to the drum
- Tilt the drum about 45% (depending on the type of stand)
- Use the non-playing hand to dampen
- Playing position will be determined by the type of stand and the size of the player

Muffling/Dampening

- Fingers, hand, knee, pads can all be used to dampen
- Use at ends of pieces, beginning of long rests, as well as other musical considerations
- Do not muffle too much – this results in a "thuddy" tone with no resonance

Stroke

- Use a direct stroke, not glancing or circular strokes
- Use a matched grip, thumbs on top
- Use the concept of "pulling sound out of drum" for maximum resonance
- Use the wrist with some arm motion
- Each stroke should have a full **body of sound**

Rolls

- Use a matched or traditional grip, depending on type of bass drum stand
- Use single stroke rolls
- Roll speed depends on the volume
    a. Soft – slow speed
    b. Medium – medium speed
    c. Loud – faster speed
- There should not be extraneous (uneven sounds) noise in the roll
- Individual strokes should not be heard
- Strive for evenness in strokes, volume, and rhythm
- The playing area will be off center and separated

Triangle – Basic Information

Selection

- Common size: 6" (good for school use); other sizes are available
- Many different materials to choose from, all of which produce different **tone colors**
- Have a variety of sizes to select from, depending on the tone color needed for music
- Use quality name brands
- Pitch should be indefinite
- Triangle clip is a necessity – can be found at hardware stores; they are used only when playing multiple percussion instruments, or playing with two triangle beaters
- String – use a thin strand with a short loop to hang the triangle from the clip
- Do not use a shoelace, leather strap, finger or anything that will dampen the sound
- Beaters come in assorted weights for different tonal colors

Playing Techniques

- Hold the triangle up to be seen and heard (about eye level)
- Form a C with the hand (right or left)
- Rest the triangle clip between thumb and index finger (middle joints) for good control – muffling is easily facilitated
- Strike at the top of triangle on the side opposite the open end, or at the bottom
- Rolls are produced by rotating the beater at the corners, striking both sides by rotating back and forth quickly, with a light stroke
- Tones should be the same, note to note – this is achieved by striking exactly the same place with the same strength every time.

Tambourine – Basic Information

Selection of Instrument

- Common size: 10" – good for most uses
- With a skin head for concert use and headless for jazz/rock use
- A wood shell is preferred
- Metal jingles come in a assortment of metals, alloys, combinations
- Skin is either glued or tacked to shell
- Jingles are either single or double rowed
- For best tones, stay with a name brand

Playing Techniques

- Hold with the thumb on top and the fingers around the side of the shell (keep the fingers out of the hole)
- Close enough to touch the bottom head with tips of the fingers
- Hold in front and at an angle – 45° for access to the head and jingles
- Cluster the tips of the fingers and thumb to use for striking; a fist can also be used to increase volume
- Use primarily a wrist stroke
- Do not move the tambourine as you strike it, hold it firmly to avoid extraneous noises
- Create different sounds and **textures** by adding/subtracting fingers
- General playing area is slightly off center
- Use the fist and/or knuckles to strike the head (center) for a sharp sound

- Rolls – two types
  a. Shake rolls – for louder and longer duration rolls; played by rotating the tambourine from side to side, beginning and ending with a finger/fist hit
  b. Thumb rolls – for shorter and softer rolls; played by placing the pad of the thumb on the head and pushing it across with enough pressure to cause friction, making the thumb "skip" across the head
- Special playing techniques
  a. Fist/knee combination – used to play fast rhythmic passages with volume; place a foot on a stool, then place the tambourine head-side down between the fist and knee and move the tambourine up and down, alternately striking the knee and fist
  b. Tambourine on a table – laid propped up on one side (1"), play with the fingers or both hands

Important Percussion Questions

Q. Why should I be concerned about the sounds produced from the percussion section?

A. Percussion is taken for granted because the sounds are easy to produce.

Q. How do I approach tonal concepts with percussion?

A. Insist that the quality, not quantity, of sound produced is the top priority.

Q. How is this achieved?

A. Through proper techniques which should be stressed at all times

Q. How important is stick/mallet quality?

A. Very important. Budget permitting, students and schools need to purchase the best sticks and mallets available. High quality mallets generally last longer, making them more cost effective. Name brands usually will work, but do not hesitate to consult with a percussion specialist.

Q. What is unique about percussion performance?

A. Because of the wide variety of instruments they play, each percussion instrument requires a certain "touch".

Q. How can a director who is a non-percussionist help a student develop the desired "touch" on a percussion instrument?

A. That, in itself is a challenge. Begin by making students aware of how it feels to produce correct and incorrect sounds. Experiment. What works for one student will not necessarily work for another. Consult percussion books, videos or clinicians. It is important that you respond to what the student plays.

Q. What do I listen for in terms of **tone colors**?

A. Percussion tone colors should have the same tonal characteristics as wind players. Individual strokes should sound the same, hand-to-hand and note-to-note. When sustaining a tone (roll), create a smooth start, good follow through and smooth ending, unless it begins and/or ends with an accent.

Q. What are some causes of extraneous noises (uneven tones)?

A.
- Sticks/mallets not matched with each other
- Sticks/mallets are not appropriate for the percussion instrument being used
- Stick/mallet height not consistent hand to hand
- Hand-to-hand position and firmness with the stick is not consistent.
- The angle of the stroke is not uniform hand to hand
- The playing area on drum or keyboard is not correct for desired tone
- The sticks or mallets too far apart
- Students are not mentally aware of the tone they are trying to produce

Q. What are some motivational techniques I can use with my percussion section?

A.
- Pay attention to what the percussionists are doing and how they are doing it.
- Have percussion sectionals outside of regular ensemble rehearsals.
- Have percussion ensembles in addition to band music.
- Special mini-assignments/research on percussion.
- Refrain from using the term "drummer" – use "percussionist."
- Help with organization during rehearsal by posting the music to be rehearsed.
- Have percussion set ups for each song.
- Insist on "a place for everything and everything in its place."
- Hold percussion ensemble recitals/concerts.
- Encourage a Percussive Arts Society – Percussion Club, etc.
- Have magazines made available (*Percussive Notes*, *Modern Drummer*, etc.)
- Create a percussion library – solos, ensembles, method books, videos, tapes, cds, etc.
- Periodically assess various percussion instruments
- Encourage the use of private teachers (a valuable resource), guest artists, clinicians

Glossary: Concepts, Terms and Techniques

Back of the Note The process of preventing air from decaying before a note is finished. By mentally placing air to the back of a note, the note has a better chance of staying resonant throughout its length.

Back to Front/Front to Back Energy Individuals or sections matching all aspects of wind playing with those performers seated behind them.

Balance (Balanced) Each instrument being heard at the tonal strength appropriate for the music. It is achieved when the conductor has assigned and prioritized the listening responsibilities. Without this information an ensemble will have a difficult time balancing.

Body of Sound The "core" between the articulated front and organized end of each note.

"Bumps" moving from note to note A phenomenon where air at the end of the note slows down, then surges at the beginning of the next note.

Capsule Any module of musical ideas–rhythmic, intervallic, stylistic, etc.

Characteristic Sounds Allowing the instrument to vibrate in the center of the harmonic series. It is a result of the engineering used to create the instruments. Every instrument will produce a characteristic sound if the balance of air, resistance of the instrument, strength of the embouchure and focus of the mind are in balance. If the body interferes with the air, a characteristic sound cannot be achieved.

Color The most mature, vibrant sound, consistent throughout all registers. Specific characteristic sounds combine to create the color of the ensemble. The conductor can create any color desired by layering the characteristic sounds of the instruments in any order.

Color Group Instruments whose characteristic sounds are similar in timbre.

Energy (Energize) A conceptual word relating to ensemble fundamentals. It can describe any aspect of musical performance (i.e., tonal resonance, line movement, specific styles, etc.) The conductor should be very specific in its use.

Ensemble Breathing The action of breathing together.

Firm Articulation A technique where the tongue shape is rounder, and touches the teeth (or reed) harder. The air becomes denser, creating the desired effect without overblowing the harmonic.

Fit Into An instrument, or group of instruments, allowing the timbre of another instrument to dominate the texture.

Focus of Articulation Directing the air behind the tongue to the center of the mouthpiece, creating a stronger front to a note, or series of notes.

Focus of Sound Balancing the air and resistance, allowing the tone quality to vibrate sympathetically within the harmonic series.

Harmonic Series The basis of all musical performance. It controls the quality of all tonal aspects of music. The performer must resonate sympathetically within the series to create an acceptable sound.

Internalized (Internalizing) The technique of a player feeling the pulse within their body. The metronome enables the player to respond aurally; the baton enables the player to respond visually; and the internalized pulse helps the student to respond physically to the movement of the phrase.

Matching (Match) Relating any aspect of playing to a specific player or section. It is a word of reference. Awareness of the conductor's desires is the key to the understanding of matching. For ensemble members to master this skill, the conductor must be very specific.

Model The performer selected by the conductor to demonstrate an aspect of a musical idea. Occasionally an entire section can be utilized the same manner.

Musical Silence A term indicating that the student's mind stays active in the music during times when they aren't actually playing. This keeps the student involved even though they are silent.

Open-throat Release The most resonant organization ending each note. The air is very deep in the body, not allowing the throat to close, or any part of the mouth to move when the sound ends. The embouchure must be perfectly still when the note is released.

Organize (Organized, Organizing) To make the ends of notes as clean and resonant as the beginnings.

Pedal Tone Any note sustained as other notes are moving. Ensembles should learn the skill of staggered-breathing to successfully create the proper function and desired effect of a pedal tone.

Pitch The actual center of sound. It can be used to describe the relationship of one note to another, one performer to another, or one section to another. However, in each instance, it is best to use the word "pitch" for only one definition. For example, only use the word "pitch" when referring to the relationship of one tone to another. Do not confuse your students by using the word "pitch" for multiple concepts.

Resonance (Resonant, Resonate) The quality beyond the core of the sound. It is the result of sympathetic vibrations within the harmonic series. Each performer should be aware of, and sensitive to, the balance of air and resistance that creates their most resonant sound. When individual performers play with resonance, the ensemble inherits a resonance of its own. There is a direct correlation between individual and ensemble resonance. Ensemble tonal resonance can only occur when the correct relationship from section to section is achieved. A layering of tonal colors will help create the ensemble tonal resonance.

Side to Side Energy An individual matching all aspects of wind playing with performers on either side.

"Silent Fingering" To silently finger/position the written music while other sections are playing.

Staggered-breathing Alternately taking breaths within a section or group, allowing a note or phrase to seemingly continue uninterrupted. This technique is most often used with extremely long notes or phrases.

Strength The degree to which a note is articulated. It is important to be consistent throughout a chosen style.

Texture The sound created when all lines of music are in balance and treated properly within the intent of the composer.

Thick Sounds The failure of instruments vibrating sympathetically with each other or within the harmonic series. The unsympathetic vibrations prevent tonal clarity.

Thin (Thinner) Sound The effect of the air stream overblowing the embouchure, or the pitch center being too high in the harmonic series.

Timbre The characteristic quality of an instrument when it is allowed to vibrate sympathetically in the harmonic series.

Tone (Tonal) Color The effect of instrument timbres being layered to create a new, more sophisticated sound.

Tonal Energy The core of a characteristic sound at its freest moment. The tonal energy can be that of an individual or a section. For example, a student can be instructed to match the tonal energy of the first chair flute player, or the trombone section can be asked to match the tonal energy of the trumpet section. Tonal energy in no way affects tonal color.

Tonal Purity The effect of a correct embouchure, correct air/resistance, and the instrument being in responsive working order.

Tonal Strength Allowing the instrument to vibrate within the harmonic series, creating the instrument's most powerful sound.

Transparency All instruments being heard in balance all of the time, satisfying the demands of the music.

Uncharacteristic Sounds The effect of the balance of air, resistance of the instrument, strength of the embouchure and focus of the mind are in disarray. No musician should wish to make an uncharacteristic sound on their instrument.

Vibrancy (Vibrant) The freedom with which an instrument, or instruments, creates its own timbre. The instrument should freely vibrate sympathetically within the harmonic series.

Vowel Sounds Shaping the tongue with vowel sound to create the tone quality the performer desires. Brass instruments use various vowel sounds depending on the register required; however, most woodwind instruments use only one vowel sound.